STEP-BY-STEP
Cooking for Christmas

STEP-BY-STEP

Cooking for Christmas

Sue Maggs

Photographs by Karl Adamson

SMITHMARK

This edition published in 1995 by
Smithmark Publishers, a division of
U.S. Media Holdings, Inc.
16 East 32nd Street
New York, NY 10016

SMITHMARK books are available for bulk purchase for sales
promotion and for premium use. For details write or call
the Manager of Special Sales, SMITHMARK Publishers Inc.,
16 East 32nd Street, New York, NY, 10016; (212) 532–6600

Produced by Anness Publishing Limited
Boundary Row Studios
1 Boundary Row
London SE1 8HP

ISBN 0-8317-3079-X

Publisher: Joanna Lorenz
Series Editor: Lindsay Porter
Designer: Lilian Lindblom
Photographer: Karl Adamson

Printed and bound in Hong Kong

CONTENTS

INTRODUCTION

Christmas is a time for celebrations, a time for entertaining family and friends and sharing the best of festive food and goodies with them. Cooking for Christmas can seem like entering a marathon, though, and not even the most avid cook wants to spend the festive season imprisoned in the kitchen: the whole family should be together as much as possible. This book includes recipes, instructions for cooking-ahead freezer tips to make the festive period as easy and as enjoyable as possible. As this is the season for entertaining, all the recipes will serve eight people; of course, the recipes can be halved or doubled, if necessary.

To make life easier for yourself over the busy Christmas period, try to prepare as much as possible in advance and finish off or reheat on the day. Planning is essential: use the suggested menus provided or make up your own menus. Use your menus to draw up shopping lists, and allow yourself plenty of time to shop. Don't forget to allow time to pick up last-minute fresh foods and try to prepare and cook as much in advance as possible. Make use of your freezer, if you have one. Desserts, pastries, and stuffings can all be made ahead and frozen.

Recipes for non meat-eaters have also been included, because so many families have one or more vegetarians to cater for at Christmas. Most of these are also very good served with any of the meat dishes as an accompaniment, and even confirmed carnivores might appreciate the variety of textures, colors and flavors provided by these interesting vegetable recipes, as a change.

On the big day, allow yourself plenty of time and don't be afraid to enlist the rest of the family to help. All this should give you the freedom to enjoy the company of family and friends.

Useful Techniques

This section contains mini-recipes and lots of tips and useful information on cooking techniques to help you sail through the holiday season. It's worth sitting down a few weeks in advance to make a few plans about what you are going to cook and when is the best time to start.

This section is arranged according to such a plan: it begins with home-made preserves to fill festive jars that will remind you of the treats to come as you make your preparations – you could even give them as presents. Then there are icings you make yourself to decorate a homemade or bought cake. Don't forget the pudding. The recipe on page 72–73 can be made up to a month in advance, and the flavor only gets better.

Once the festive season gets under way, there are plenty of opportunities for parties and get-togethers of all sorts. The recipes in the Cold Buffets chapter are designed for hassle-free entertaining for large numbers. In this section you will find ideas for

cocktail snacks that will supplement the buffet or be perfect for when the neighbours drop by. Ideas for Christmas drinks are also given, including low- and non-alcoholic ideas.

On Christmas Day itself, the information on turkey and its accompaniments will give you all you need for a triumphant celebratory dinner. Follow the turkey with your pudding, accompanied by one of the delicious sweet sauces.

Lastly in this section are some suggested menus for all kinds of occasions over the holiday season. Use them to take the anxiety out of planning, or as a starting point for your own ideas.

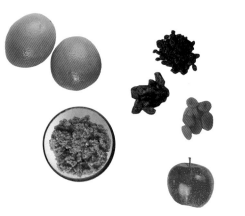

Spiced Cranberry and Orange Relish

This is excellent with roast turkey, goose or duck.

Makes about 1 lb

INGREDIENTS
1½ cups fresh cranberries
1 onion, finely chopped
⅔ cup port
½ cup superfine sugar
finely grated rind and juice of 1 orange
½ tsp English mustard powder
¼ tsp ground ginger
¼ tsp ground cinnamon
1 tsp cornstarch
⅓ cup raisins

2 Mix the orange juice, mustard powder, spices and cornstarch together. Stir them into the cranberries.

1 Put the cranberries, onion, port and sugar in a pan. Cook gently for 10 minutes, until tender.

3 Add the raisins and orange rind. Allow to thicken over the heat, stirring with a wooden spoon and then simmer for 2 minutes. Cool, cover and chill ready for serving.

Curried Fruit Chutney

Make this well ahead of Christmas, to serve with cold sliced turkey and ham.

Makes about 2½ lb

INGREDIENTS
1⅓ cups dried
  apricots
1⅓ cups dried peaches
1⅓ cups dates, pitted
1⅓ cups raisins
1–2 garlic cloves, crushed
1 generous cup light brown
  sugar
1¼ cups white malt vinegar
1¼ cups water
1 tsp salt
2 tsp mild curry powder

2 Chop or mince the mixture coarsely in batches in a food processor.

1 Put all the ingredients in a large pan, cover and simmer very gently for 10–15 minutes, or until tender.

3 Spoon into clean jelly jars. Seal the jars and label them. Store in a cool place for 4 weeks before using.

Ginger, Date, and Apple Chutney

Make this well ahead and store it in airtight jars. Serve with cold sliced meats or pies.

Makes about 3½ lb

INGREDIENTS
1 lb cooking apples
1 lb dates
1⅓ cups dried apricots
4 oz crystallized ginger,
  chopped
1–2 garlic cloves, crushed
1⅓ cups sultanas
1 generous cup light brown
  sugar
1 tsp salt
1¼ cups white malt vinegar

2 Put all the fruit together in a large pan, with the remaining ingredients. Cover and simmer gently for 10–15 minutes, or until tender.

1 Peel, core and chop the apples. Pit the dates and chop them roughly. Chop the apricots.

3 Spoon into clean jelly jars. Seal the jars and label them. Store in a cool place for 4 weeks before using.

Lining a Cake Pan

Rich, fruity Christmas cakes must be baked in a lined pan. The technique is very straightforward.

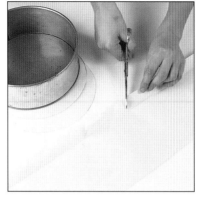

1 Place the cake pan on a double piece of wax paper, draw around the base of the pan and cut out two circles to fit inside the pan.

2 Measure the circumference of the pan with a piece of string and cut a double strip of wax paper slightly longer than the circumference and at least 3 in taller than the pan. Fold over 1 in along one long side. Cut diagonal slits in the folded-over part, up to the fold line.

3 Grease the pan. Place one circle of paper in the base of the pan. Fit the double-strip around the pan, neatly arranging the snipped edge over the bottom of the pan so it fits flat. Place the second circle of wax paper on top, to make a smooth base.

Fondant Icing

This icing can be used for modeling decorations as well as covering a cake.

Makes enough to cover an 8 in round cake

INGREDIENTS
4 tbsp water
1 tbsp powdered gelatin
2 tsp liquid glucose
5 cups confectioner's sugar

1 Put the water in a small bowl and sprinkle the gelatin over. Let soak for 2 minutes. Place the bowl in a pan of hot water and leave to dissolve over a very gentle heat.

2 Remove the bowl from the hot water and add the liquid glucose to the dissolved gelatin.

3 Sift the confectioner's sugar into a bowl and add the gelatin mixture. Mix and then knead to a smooth paste. Wrap in plastic wrap until ready to use.

Almond Paste

Use almond paste as a base for royal or fondant icing. It will help to keep the cake moist.

Makes enough to cover an 8 in round cake

INGREDIENTS
4 cups ground almonds
⅞ cup superfine sugar
1½ cups confectioner's sugar
1 tsp lemon juice
¼ tsp almond extract
1 egg

1 Sift the almonds, superfine sugar and confectioner's sugar together into a bowl.

2 With a fork, beat the lemon juice, almond extract and egg together in a small bowl. Stir them into the dry ingredients.

3 Knead together until smooth and wrap in plastic wrap until needed.

Royal Icing

This icing will dry very hard and is a wonderful covering for cakes.

Makes enough to cover an 8 in round cake

INGREDIENTS
2 egg whites
1 tsp lemon juice
1 tsp glycerin (optional)
1 lb confectioner's sugar

1 In a large bowl, beat the egg whites, lemon juice and glycerin (if using) together with a fork.

2 Sift in enough confectioner's sugar to make a thick paste.

3 Using a wooden spoon, beat in the remaining confectioner's sugar until the icing forms stiff peaks. Cover with plastic wrap until ready to use.

Nutty Cheese Balls

These tasty morsels are perfect for nibbling with drinks.

Makes 32

INGREDIENTS
4 oz cream cheese
4 oz Roquefort cheese
1 cup finely chopped walnuts
chopped fresh parsley, to coat
paprika, to coat
salt and freshly ground black pepper

1 Beat the two cheeses together until smooth using an electric beater.

2 Stir in the chopped walnuts and season with salt and pepper.

3 Shape into small balls (about a rounded teaspoonful each). Chill on a baking sheet until firm.

4 Roll half the balls in the chopped parsley and half in the paprika. Serve on toothpicks.

Salami and Olive Cheese Wedges

Genoa salami is delicious with the olives.

Makes 24

INGREDIENTS
8 oz cream cheese
1 tsp paprika
½ tsp English mustard powder
2 tbsp stuffed green olives,
    chopped
8 oz sliced salami
sliced olives, to garnish

1 Beat the cream cheese with the paprika and mustard and mix well. Stir in the chopped olives.

2 Spread the salami slices with the olive mixture and stack five slices on top of each other. Wrap in plastic wrap and chill until firm. With a sharp knife, cut each stack into four wedges. Garnish with additional sliced olives and serve with a toothpick through each wedge, to hold the slices together.

Spiced Mixed Nuts

Spices are a delicious addition to mixed roasted nuts.

Makes 2 cups

INGREDIENTS
⅔ cup brazil nuts
⅔ cup cashew nuts
⅔ cup almonds
1 tsp garam masala
½ tsp ground coriander
½ tsp salt
2 tbsp butter, melted

1 Preheat the oven to 350°F. Put all the nuts and spices and the salt on to a baking tray and mix well.

2 Pour the melted butter over and bake for 10–15 minutes, stirring until golden brown.

3 Drain on paper towels and allow to cool before serving.

Herby Cheese Crackers

Use a selection of festive shapes for cutting out these crackers.

Makes 32

INGREDIENTS
3 cups all-purpose flour
½ tsp cayenne pepper
1 tsp English mustard powder
¾ cup butter
6 oz sharp Cheddar cheese, grated finely
1 tbsp mixed dried herbs
1 egg, beaten
salt and freshly ground black pepper

1 Preheat the oven to 400°F. Sift the flour, cayenne pepper and mustard powder together into a bowl or food processor.

2 Rub the butter into the flour and add the cheese, herbs and seasoning. Stir in the beaten egg to bind, and knead to a smooth dough.

3 On a lightly floured work surface, roll the dough out thinly. Stamp it into small biscuits with cutters. Bake for 10–15 minutes, or until golden. Cool on a wire rack. Store in an airtight container.

Mulled Red Wine

Excellent to serve on a cold winter's evening; it will really get the party started.

Makes 2½ cups

INGREDIENTS
1 bottle red wine
⅓ cup light brown sugar
2 cinnamon sticks
1 lemon, sliced
4 whole cloves
⅔ cup brandy or port
lemon slices, to serve

2 Strain to remove the spices and lemon slices.

1 Put all the ingredients, except the brandy or port, into a large pan. Bring the wine to a boil to dissolve the sugar. Remove from the heat, cover the pan and leave it to stand for 5 minutes, to allow the flavors to infuse.

3 Add the brandy and serve warm, with a fresh slice of lemon.

Sparkling Cider Punch

This is a very refreshing, sparkling drink, best served as cold as possible.

Makes 10½ cups

INGREDIENTS
1 orange
1 lemon
1 apple
4 cups sparkling cider, chilled
4 cups lemonade, chilled
2½ cups apple juice, chilled
fresh mint sprigs, to serve

2 Add the cider, lemonade and apple juice. Serve cold with sprigs of fresh mint.

1 Slice all the fruit into a large bowl.

Spiced Fruit Cocktail

This non-alcoholic fruit drink is a real treat.

Makes 8¾ cups

INGREDIENTS
2½ cups orange juice,
   chilled
1¼ cups pineapple juice,
   chilled
pared rind and juice of 1 lemon
4 whole cloves
1 cinnamon stick, broken into pieces
4 tbsp superfine sugar
orange slices
ice cubes
2½ cups sparkling mineral water,
   chilled
2½ cups ginger ale, chilled

1 Mix the orange and pineapple juices together in a large bowl. Add the lemon rind and juice, spices and sugar. Chill.

2 Put the orange slices and ice cubes in a serving bowl. Strain the fruit juice mixture into the bowl. Add the mineral water and ginger ale.

Fruit Punch

This is a quick punch to assemble. Make sure that all the ingredients are well chilled.

Makes 10¼ cups

INGREDIENTS
1 bottle white wine, chilled
1 bottle red wine, chilled
3 tbsp orange-flavored liqueur
1 orange, cut in quarters and sliced
seedless grapes
ice cubes
4 cups sparkling lemonade

2 Add the orange pieces, grapes and ice and finally the sparkling lemonade.

1 Empty the wines and liqueur into a large bowl.

Prune, Orange and Nut Stuffing

You could also finely chop the reserved turkey liver and mix it into this stuffing.

Serves 8 (enough to stuff a 10 lb turkey)

INGREDIENTS
1 cup pitted prunes
4 tbsp red wine or sherry
1 onion, finely chopped
2 tbsp butter
4 cups fresh white bread crumbs
finely grated rind of 1 orange
2 eggs, beaten
2 tbsp chopped fresh parsley
1 tbsp mixed dried herbs
large pinch of ground allspice
large pinch of grated nutmeg
1 cup chopped walnuts or
   pecans
2 celery stalks, finely chopped
salt and freshly ground black pepper

1 Put the prunes and red wine or sherry in a small pan, cover and simmer gently until tender. Set aside to cool.

2 Cook the onion gently in the butter until tender, about 10 minutes.

3 Cut each prune into four pieces. Mix all the ingredients in a large bowl and season well with salt and pepper.

Rice, Mushroom and Leek Stuffing

The rice gives this stuffing a crumbly, light texture.

Serves 8 (enough to stuff a 10 lb turkey)

INGREDIENTS
½ cup rice
2 tbsp butter
3 cups leeks, washed and sliced
2½ cups mushrooms, chopped
2 celery stalks, finely chopped
½ cup chopped walnuts
1 egg, beaten
4 tbsp chopped fresh parsley
2 tsp dried thyme
finely grated rind of 1 lemon
2 cooking apples, peeled, cored and
   diced
salt and freshly ground black pepper

2 Mix all the remaining ingredients thoroughly together in a large bowl and season with salt and pepper.

1 Cook the rice in plenty of boiling, salted water for 12 minutes until tender. Drain the rice thoroughly and let it cool. Melt the butter in a frying-pan and cook the leeks and mushrooms until tender. Increase the heat and cook to evaporate any remaining moisture in the pan. Set aside to cool.

3 Add the rice, and the leek and mushroom mixture to the bowl and mix together thoroughly.

Making Bacon Rolls

If you want to wrap pitted prunes or chicken livers inside each strip cut the bacon strips in half after stretching them.

1 Remove the rind from the rashers of bacon and stretch them with the back of a large knife.

2 Roll the strips up neatly.

3 Skewer the bacon rolls with toothpicks. Broil the rolls until crisp, turning them halfway through cooking.

Roasting Potatoes

Floury potatoes make the best crisp roast potatoes. Garlic or rosemary can be added to the oil, to flavor the potatoes during cooking.

1 Preheat the oven to 400°F. Peel the potatoes and cut large potatoes in half. Parboil them for 10 minutes. Drain. Score the surface of each potato with a fork. Roll them in flour and tap them to remove any excess. Heat 1 in olive oil in a shallow roasting pan until smoking hot.

2 Put the potatoes in the hot oil and baste them to coat them in oil. Roast for about an hour.

3 Baste and turn the potatoes twice during cooking. Drain them on paper towels and sprinkle them with salt.

17

Carving a Turkey

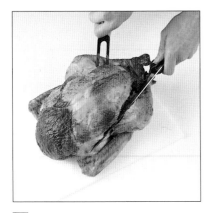

1 First remove the leg, by cutting the skin between the breast and leg. Press the leg flat, to expose the joint. Cut between the bones through the joint.

2 Cut the leg in two, through the joint.

3 Carve the leg into slices.

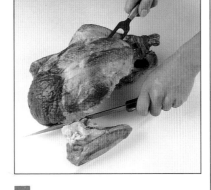

4 Remove the wing, cutting through the joint in the same way as for the leg.

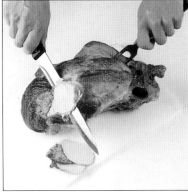

5 Carve the breast in thin slices, starting at the front of the breast. Then carve slices from the back of the breast, alternating the slices between front and back, until all the breast has been carved.

Times for Roasting Turkey

When choosing a turkey for Christmas, you should allow about 1 lb of dressed (plucked and oven-ready) bird per person. A good sized turkey to buy for Christmas is 10 lb. This will serve about 12 people, with leftovers for the following day.

Thaw a frozen turkey, still in its bag, on a plate at room temperature (65–70°F) until the legs are flexible and there are no ice crystals in the cavity of the bird. Remove the giblets from the cavity as soon as the bird has thawed enough.

Oven-ready weight	Thawing time	Number of servings	Cooking time
8 lb	18 hours	8–10 people	2½–3½ hours
10 lb	19 hours	12–14 people	3½–4 hours
12 lb	20 hours	16–18 people	3¾–4½ hours
14 lb	24 hours	18–20 people	4–5 hours

These times apply to a turkey weighed after stuffing and at room temperature. Cook in a moderate oven, 350°F, covered with butter and bacon strips and loosely covered with foil.

To test whether the turkey is fully cooked, push a skewer into the thickest part of the leg and press the flesh; the juices should run clear and free from any blood. The legs take longer than the breast to cook; keep the breast covered with foil until the legs are cooked. The foil can be removed for the final hour of cooking, to brown and crisp the skin. The turkey should be basted with the juices from the roasting pan, every hour of cooking.

Plan for the turkey to be ready 15–20 minutes before you want to serve dinner. Remove it from the oven and allow the flesh to relax before carving it.

Brandy or Rum Butter

Serve with Christmas pudding or mince pies.

Makes about ¾ cup

INGREDIENTS
6 tbsp unsalted butter
6 tbsp superfine sugar
finely grated rind of 1 small orange
3 tbsp brandy or rum

1 Whisk the butter, sugar and orange rind together until soft and fluffy.

2 Gradually whisk in the brandy or rum. Chill until ready to serve.

Whisky Sauce

This is another delicious accompaniment to Christmas pudding or mince pies.

Makes about 2½ cups

INGREDIENTS
2 tbsp cornstarch
2½ cups milk
2 tbsp superfine sugar
4 tbsp whisky
grated nutmeg

1 In a small bowl, mix the cornstarch with 1 tbsp of the milk to make a smooth paste.

2 Bring the remaining milk to a boil, remove from the heat and pour a little on to the cornstarch mixture and mix the cornstarch into the pan.

3 Return to the heat, stirring constantly until thickened. Simmer for 2 minutes. Turn off the heat and add the sugar and whisky. Pour into a serving pitcher and sprinkle with the grated nutmeg.

SUGGESTED MENUS

Christmas Dinner for 8 People

Cheese and Pesto Pastries

Roast Turkey, stuffing balls, sausages,
Bacon Rolls and gravy

Roast Potatoes and Brussels Sprouts
with Chestnuts and Carrots

Steamed Christmas Pudding
with Whisky Sauce

Vegetarian Christmas Dinner for 8 People

Christmas Salad with mini bread rolls

Cheese and Spinach Quiche or
Vegetarian Christmas Pie

Vegetable Crumble or Brussels Sprouts with
Chestnuts and Carrots

Crunchy Apple and Almond Flan

New Year's Eve Party for 8 People

Smoked Salmon Salad

Roast Goose with Caramelized Apples,
with Port and Orange Gravy

Gratin Dauphinois and Sweet and Sour
Red Cabbage

Chocolate and Chestnut Yule Log

Hot Supper for 12 People

Roquefort Tartlets and Stilton
with Herbs Spread and Melba toast

Spiced Lamb with Fruit Pilaf

Sweet and Sour Red Cabbage

Iced Praline Torte and Ruby Fruit Salad

Boxing Day Lunch for 12 People

Warm Shrimp Salad with
herb and garlic bread

Baked Country Ham with Cumberland Sauce

Vegetable Gnocchi

Deluxe Mincemeat Tart

Cold Buffet Lunch for 12 People

Layered Salmon Terrine

Fillet of Beef with Ratatouille

Turkey Rice Salad

Ginger Trifle and Almond Mincemeat Tartlets

Countdown to Christmas

This at-a-glance timetable will help you plan and organize your Christmas cooking. If you have chosen your menu from one of those suggested previously, the table below suggests when the components may be prepared.

Late Autumn

Make preserves and relishes such as Cranberry and Orange Relish or Curried Fruit Chutney to serve with cold meats.

November

Second week

Make Moist and Rich Christmas Cake.

Third week

Feed Moist and Rich Christmas Cake (optional).

Fourth week

Make Christmas Pudding.
Decide on Christmas dinner menu.
Order turkey, goose, beef or ham.
Continue to feed Moist and Rich Christmas Cake (optional).

December

First week

Make Light Jeweled Fruit Cake.
Make mincemeat for Deluxe Mincemeat Tart.
Continue to feed Moist and Rich Christmas Cake (optional).
Compile complete shopping list for main Christmas meals under headings for different stores, or for the various counters at the supermarket.
Continue to add to list throughout the week.

Second week

Make Almond Paste to cover Moist and Rich Christmas Cake.
Shop for dry goods such as rice, dried fruits and flour.
Order special bread requirements.
Order milk, cream and other dairy produce.
Make Brandy or Rum Butter.

Third week

Make Cheese and Pesto Pastries and other pastry-type cocktail savories and freeze.
Cover Moist and Rich Christmas Cake with royal icing, leave one day, then cover and store.

Fourth week

Shop for chilled ingredients.
Buy wines and other drinks.

21 December

Check thawing time for frozen turkey, duck, beef or other meat.
Large turkeys (25 lb) need 86 hours (3½ days) to thaw in the refrigerator, or 40 hours at room temperature.
Make a note to take the meat from the freezer at the appropriate time.

23 December

Shop for fresh vegetables, if not possible to do so on 24 December.
Make Cheese and Spinach Quiche and freeze, if not making on Christmas Day.
Make Crunchy Apple and Almond Flan.

24 December

Shop for fresh vegetables, if possible.
Assemble Christmas Salad and refrigerate dressing separately.
Make stuffing for poultry.
Cook poultry giblets to make gravy.
Defrost Cheese and Pesto Pastries.
Prepare Bacon Rolls by threading them on to toothpicks.
Make Whisky Sauce to serve with Christmas Pudding.

Christmas Day

This timetable is planned for Christmas Dinner to be served at 2.00pm. If you wish to serve it at a different time, please adjust the times accordingly.

Stuff poultry. Make forcemeat balls with any leftover stuffing, or spoon it into greased ovenproof dishes.
Set table, if not already done.

Put steamer or large saucepan on cooker and bring water to a boil.
Put Christmas Pudding on to steam.

To cook a 10 lb turkey

9.05am	Set oven to 425°F.
9.25am	Put turkey in oven.
9.45am	Reduce heat to 350°F.

Baste turkey now and at frequent intervals.

12.15pm	Put potatoes around meat. Remove foil from turkey and baste again.
12.45pm	Turn the potatoes. Increase heat to 400°F. Put any dishes of stuffing in oven.
1.45pm	Remove turkey and potatoes from oven, put on heated dish, cover with foil and keep warm. Make gravy and broil bacon rolls.

To cook vegetarian menu

11.15am	Make pastry for Cheese and Spinach Quiche, if not cooking from frozen. (If you are making Christmas Pie, begin 20 minutes earlier to allow time to chill the assembled pie.)
11.45am	Put pastry in the fridge and chill. Prepare sprouts for Brussels Sprouts with Chestnuts and Carrots.
12.15pm	Preheat oven for Cheese and Spinach Quiche. Remove pastry from fridge and assemble. (For Christmas Pie, chill assembled dish for 20 minutes before baking. Preheat oven 10 minutes before removing pie from fridge.)
1.00pm	Put quiche or pie in oven.
1.20pm	Simmer chestnuts for 10 minutes.
1.30pm	Simmer sprouts for 5 minutes.
1.35pm	Simmer carrots for 5 minutes.
1.40pm	Gently reheat all vegetables together.
1.45pm	Remove quiche or pie from oven.
2.00pm	Serve first course.

Cheese and Pesto Pastries

These pastries can be made ahead and frozen uncooked. Freeze them in a single layer and then transfer them to a freezer-proof container. To serve, arrange the pastries on baking trays, brush them with oil and bake from frozen for 5–10 minutes longer than the recommended time.

Serves 8

INGREDIENTS
8 oz frozen chopped spinach
2 tbsp pine nuts
4 tbsp pesto sauce
4 oz Gruyère cheese
½ cup grated Parmesan cheese
2 × 10 oz packet of frozen filo pastry,
    thawed
2 tbsp olive oil
salt and freshly ground black pepper,
    to taste

Parmesan

olive oil

spinach

pesto sauce

filo pastry

pine nuts

1 Preheat the oven to 375°F. Prepare the filling; put the frozen spinach into a pan, and heat gently, breaking it up as it defrosts. Increase the heat to evaporate any excess moisture. Transfer to a bowl and cool slightly.

2 Put the pine nuts into a frying pan and stir over a very low heat until they are lightly toasted. Chop them and add them to the spinach, with the pesto and Gruyère and Parmesan cheeses. Season to taste.

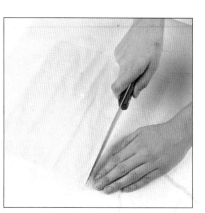

3 Unwrap the filo pastry and cover it with plastic wrap and a damp dish towel (to prevent it from drying out). Take one sheet at a time and cut it into 2 in wide strips. Brush each strip with oil.

4 Put a teaspoon of filling on one end of each strip of pastry. Fold the end over in a triangle, enclosing the filling.

5 Continue to fold the triangle over and over again until the end of the strip is reached. Repeat with the other strips, until all the filling has been used up.

6 Place the pastries on baking trays, brush them with oil and bake for 20–25 minutes, or until golden brown. Cool on a wire rack. Serve warm.

Christmas Salad

A light first course that can be prepared ahead and assembled just before serving.

Serves 8

INGREDIENTS
mixed red and green lettuce leaves
2 sweet pink grapefruit
1 large or 2 small avocados, peeled
  and cubed

FOR THE DRESSING
6 tbsp light olive oil
2 tbsp red wine vinegar
1 garlic clove, crushed
1 tsp Dijon mustard
salt and freshly ground black pepper

FOR THE CARAMELIZED ORANGE PEEL
4 oranges
4 tbsp superfine sugar
4 tbsp cold water

lettuce leaves

red wine vinegar

oranges

avocados

grapefruit

olive oil

1 To make the caramelized peel, using a vegetable peeler, remove the rind from the oranges in thin strips and reserve the fruit. Scrape away the white pith from the underside of the rind with a sharp knife, and cut the rind in fine shreds.

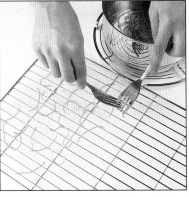

2 Put the sugar and water in a small pan and heat gently until the sugar has dissolved. Then add the shreds of orange rind, increase the heat and boil steadily for 5 minutes, until the rind is tender. Using two forks, remove the orange rind from the syrup and spread it out on a wire rack to dry. (This can be done the day before). Reserve the syrup to add to the dressing.

3 Wash and dry the lettuce and tear the leaves into bite-sized pieces. Wrap them in a clean, damp dish towel and keep them in the fridge. Cut the pith off the oranges and grapefruit. Holding the fruit over a bowl to catch any juice, cut them into segments, removing all the pith.

4 Put all the dressing ingredients into a screw-top jar and shake the jar vigorously to emulsify the dressing. Add the reserved orange-flavored syrup and adjust the seasoning to taste. Arrange the salad ingredients on individual plates with the avocados, spoon over the dressing and scatter on the caramelized peel.

Warm Shrimp Salad with Spicy Marinade

The ingredients can be prepared in advance; if you do this, cook the shrimp and bacon just before serving, spoon over the salad and serve with hot herb and garlic bread.

Serves 8

INGREDIENTS
8 oz large, cooked, shelled shrimp
8 oz smoked lean bacon,
    chopped
mixed lettuce leaves
2 tbsp chopped fresh chives

FOR THE LEMON AND CHILI MARINADE
1 garlic clove, crushed
finely grated rind of 1 lemon
1 tbsp lemon juice
4 tbsp olive oil
¼ tsp chili paste, or a large pinch
    dried ground chili
1 tbsp light soy sauce
salt and freshly ground black pepper

1 In a glass bowl, mix the shrimp with the garlic, lemon rind and juice, 3 tbsp of oil, the chili paste and soy sauce. Season with salt and pepper. Cover with plastic wrap and let marinate for at least one hour.

shrimp
chili paste
lettuce leaves
chives
lemon
soy sauce
garlic
bacon

2 Gently cook the bacon in the remaining oil until crisp. Drain on a paper towel.

3 Wash and dry the lettuce, tear the leaves into bite-sized pieces and arrange them in individual bowls or on plates.

4 Just before serving, put the shrimp with their marinade into a large frying-pan, bring to a boil, add the bacon and cook for one minute. Spoon over the salad and sprinkle with chopped chives. Serve immediately.

Smoked Salmon Salad

To save time, prepare all the ingredients in advance and assemble them on the plates just before serving. The dressing can be made the day before and kept in the fridge.

Serves 8

INGREDIENTS
4 thin slices white bread
oil, for frying
paprika, for dusting
mixed lettuce leaves
1 oz Parmesan cheese
8 oz smoked salmon or trout, thinly
    sliced
1 lemon

FOR THE VINAIGRETTE DRESSING
6 tbsp olive oil
2 tbsp red wine vinegar
1 garlic clove, crushed
1 tsp Dijon mustard
1 tsp honey
1 tbsp chopped fresh parsley
½ tsp fresh thyme
2 tsp capers, chopped
salt and freshly ground black pepper

lettuce leaves

lemon

paprika

bread

smoked salmon

2 With a small star-shaped cutter, stamp out as many shapes from the slices of bread as possible. Heat 1 in oil in a shallow frying-pan until the oil is almost smoking (test it with a cube of bread, it should sizzle on the surface and brown within 30 seconds). Fry the croûtons, in small batches, until golden brown all over. Remove the croûtons with a slotted spoon and let them drain on paper towels. Dust with paprika and let cool.

1 First make the dressing. Put all the ingredients into a screw-top jar and shake the jar well to emulsify the dressing. Season to taste.

3 Wash the lettuce, dry the leaves and tear them into small bite-sized pieces. Wrap in a clean, damp dish towel and keep the lettuce in the fridge until ready to serve.

4 Cut the Parmesan cheese into shavings with a vegetable peeler. Put into a dish and cover with plastic wrap.

5 Cut the salmon or trout into ½ in strips no more than 2 in long. Cut the lemon into eight thin wedges.

6 To assemble the salad, arrange the lettuce on individual plates, scatter over the Parmesan shavings and arrange the salmon strips on top. Shake the dressing vigorously to emulsify it again and spoon a little over each salad. Scatter over the croûtons, place a lemon wedge on the side of each plate and serve immediately.

Roquefort Tartlets

These can be made in shallow tartlet pans to serve hot as a first course. You could also make them in mini pie pans, to serve warm as bite-sized snacks with a drink before a meal.

Makes 12

INGREDIENTS
1½ cups all-purpose flour
large pinch of salt
½ cup butter
1 egg yolk
2 tbsp cold water

FOR THE FILLING
1 tbsp butter
1 tbsp all-purpose flour
⅔ cup milk
4 oz Roquefort cheese, crumbled
⅔ cup heavy cream
½ tsp dried mixed herbs
3 egg yolks
salt and freshly ground black pepper

flour

milk

Roquefort

butter

eggs

1 To make the pastry, sift the flour and salt into a bowl and rub the butter into the flour until it resembles bread crumbs. Mix the egg yolk with the water and stir into the flour to make a soft dough. Knead until smooth, wrap in plastic wrap and chill for 30 minutes. (You can also make the dough in a food processor.)

2 Melt the butter, stir in the flour and then the milk. Boil to thicken, stirring continuously. Off the heat beat in the cheese and season. Cool. Bring the cream and herbs to a boil. Reduce to 2 tbsp. Beat into the sauce with the eggs.

3 Preheat the oven to 375°F. On a lightly floured work surface, roll out the pastry ⅛ in thick. Stamp out rounds with a fluted cutter and use to line your chosen tartlet pans.

4 Divide the filling between the tartlets; they should be filled only two-thirds full. Stamp out smaller fluted rounds or star shapes for the tops and lay on top of each tartlet. Bake for 20–25 minutes, or until puffed and golden brown.

Stilton with Herbs Spread and Melba Toast

Make this the day before and serve it in small ramekins with the crisp Melba toast, as an hors d'oeuvre or first course. The Melba toast will keep in an airtight container for a day or two.

Serves 8

INGREDIENTS
8 oz blue Stilton or other blue cheese
4 oz cream cheese
1 tbsp port
1 tbsp chopped fresh parsley
1 tbsp chopped fresh chives, plus
    extra to garnish
½ cup finely chopped walnuts
salt and freshly ground black pepper

FOR THE MELBA TOAST
12 thin slices white bread

Stilton

walnuts   *bread*

parsley

cream cheese

chives

1 Put the Stilton, cream cheese and port into a bowl or food processor and beat until smooth.

2 Stir in the remaining ingredients and season with salt and pepper to taste.

3 Spoon into individual ramekins and level the tops. Cover with plastic wrap and chill until firm. Sprinkle with chopped chives before serving. To make the melba toast, preheat the oven to 350°F. Toast the bread lightly on both sides.

4 While the toast is still hot, cut off the crusts, and cut each slice horizontally in two. While the bread is still warm, place it in a single layer on baking trays and bake for 10–15 minutes, until golden brown and crisp. Continue with the remaining slices in the same way. Serve warm with the Stilton spread.

Baked Country Ham with Cumberland Sauce

Serve this delicious cooked meat and sauce either hot or cold. The country ham must be soaked overnight before cooking to remove any strong salty flavor resulting from the curing process.

Serves 8–10

INGREDIENTS
5 lb smoked or unsmoked country
    ham
1 onion
1 carrot
1 celery stalk
bouquet garni sachet
6 peppercorns

FOR THE GLAZE
whole cloves
4 tbsp light brown or demerara sugar
2 tbsp corn syrup
1 tsp English mustard powder

FOR THE CUMBERLAND SAUCE
juice and shredded rind of 1 orange
2 tbsp lemon juice
½ cup port or red wine
4 tbsp red currant jelly

1 Soak the ham overnight in a cool place in plenty of cold water to cover. Discard this water. Put the ham into a large pan and cover it again with more cold water. Bring the water to a boil slowly and skim any scum from the surface with a slotted spoon.

2 Add the vegetables and seasonings, cover, and simmer very gently for 2 hours. (The meat can also be cooked in the oven at 350°F. Allow 30 minutes per lb.)

3 Leave the meat to cool in the liquid for 30 minutes. Then remove it from the liquid and strip off the skin neatly with the help of a knife (use rubber gloves if the ham is too hot to handle).

4 Score the fat in diamonds with a sharp knife and stick a clove in the center of each diamond.

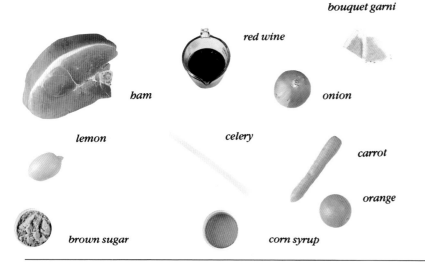

bouquet garni

red wine

ham

onion

lemon

celery

carrot

orange

brown sugar

corn syrup

5 Preheat the oven to 350°F. Put the sugar, corn syrup and mustard powder in a small pan and heat gently to melt them. Place the ham in a roasting pan and spoon over the glaze. Bake it until golden brown, about 20 minutes. Put it under a hot broiler, if necessary, to get a good color. Allow to stand in a warm place for about 15 minutes before carving (this allows the flesh to relax and makes carving much easier).

6 For the sauce, put the orange and lemon juice into a pan with the port and red currant jelly, and heat gently to melt the jelly. Pour boiling water over the orange rind, drain, and add to the sauce. Cook gently for 2 minutes. Serve the sauce hot, in a sauce boat.

Roast Turkey

Serve with stuffing balls, bacon rolls, roast potatoes, Brussels sprouts and gravy.

Serves 8

INGREDIENTS

10 lb oven-ready turkey, with giblets
   (thawed overnight if frozen)
1 large onion, peeled and stuck with 6
   whole cloves
4 tbsp butter, softened
10 sausages
salt and freshly ground black pepper

FOR THE STUFFING

8 oz lean bacon, chopped
1 large onion, finely chopped
1 lb bulk pork sausage
⅓ cup rolled oats
2 tbsp chopped fresh parsley
2 tsp dried mixed herbs
1 large egg, beaten
⅔ cup dried apricots, finely
   chopped

FOR THE GRAVY

2 tbsp all-purpose flour
1⅞ cups giblet stock

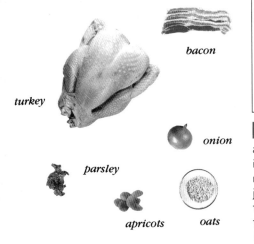

turkey

bacon

onion

parsley

apricots   oats

1 Preheat the oven to 400°F. Adjust the oven shelves to allow for the size of the turkey. For the stuffing, cook the bacon and onion gently in a pan until the bacon is crisp and the onion tender. Transfer to a large bowl and mix in all the remaining stuffing ingredients. Season well with salt and pepper.

4 Spread the turkey with the butter and season it with salt and pepper. Cover it loosely with foil and cook it for 30 minutes. Baste the turkey with the pan juices. Then lower the oven temperature to 350°F and cook for the remainder of the calculated time (about 3½ hours for a 10 lb bird). Baste it every 30 minutes or so.

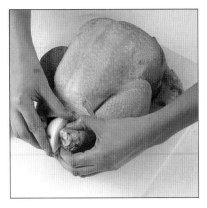

2 Stuff the neck-end of the turkey only, tuck the flap of skin under and secure it with a small skewer or stitch it with thread (do not over-stuff the turkey or the skin will burst during cooking). Reserve any remaining stuffing.

5 With wet hands, shape the remaining stuffing into small balls or pack it into a greased ovenproof dish. Cook in the oven for 20 minutes, or until golden brown and crisp. About 20 minutes before the end of cooking put the sausages into an ovenproof dish and put them in the oven. Remove the foil from the turkey for the last hour of cooking and baste it. The turkey is cooked if the juices run clear when the thickest part of the thigh has been pierced with a skewer.

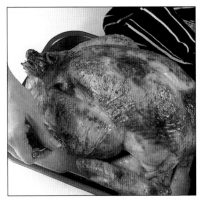

3 Put the whole onion studded with cloves in the body cavity of the turkey and tie the legs together. Weigh the stuffed bird and calculate the cooking time; allow 15 minutes per 1 lb plus 15 minutes over. Place the turkey in a large roasting pan.

6 Transfer the turkey to a serving plate, cover it with foil and let it stand for 15 minutes before carving. To make the gravy, spoon off the fat from the roasting pan, leaving the meat juices. Blend in the flour and cook for 2 minutes. Gradually stir in the stock and bring to a boil. Check the seasoning and pour into a sauce boat. Remove the skewer or string and pour any juices into the gravy. To serve, surround the turkey with sausages, bacon rolls and stuffing balls.

Roast Duck with Orange

Most of the meat on a duck is on the breast. It is easier to cut the whole breast off each side of the carcass and slice it thinly on a board. The ducks can be cooked the day before, sliced and reheated in some of the gravy. The remaining gravy, with the orange segments, can be reheated gently just before serving.

Serves 8

INGREDIENTS

4 oranges, segmented, with rind and
   juice reserved
2 × 5 lb oven-ready ducks, with
   giblets
salt and freshly ground black pepper

FOR THE SAUCE
2 tbsp flour
1¼ cups giblet stock
⅔ cup port or red wine
1 tbsp red currant jelly

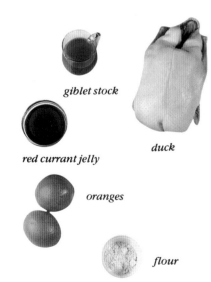

giblet stock

red currant jelly

duck

oranges

flour

1 Preheat the oven to 350°F. Tie the orange rind with string and place it inside the cavities of the ducks.

2 Place the ducks on a rack in a roasting pan, season and cook for 30 minutes per 1 lb (about 2½ hours), until the flesh is tender and the juices run clear. Pour off the fat into a bowl halfway through the cooking time.

3 Transfer the ducks to a carving board and remove the orange rind from the cavities. To make the sauce, remove any fat from the roasting pan, leaving the sediment and juices behind. Sprinkle in the flour and cook gently for 2 minutes. Blend in the rest of the ingredients and reserved orange rind, coarsely chopped. Bring to a boil and simmer for 10 minutes; then strain into a pan, and add the orange segments, with their juice.

4 To carve the ducks, remove the legs and wings, cutting through the joints. Cut the two end joints off the wings and discard them. Cut the breast meat off the carcass in one piece and slice it thinly. Arrange the slices on a warm serving plate with the legs and the wing joints. Spoon some of the hot sauce over and serve the rest separately in a sauce boat.

Spiced Lamb with Fruit Pilaf

This wonderfully rich and spicy dish is excellent for a New Year's Eve party. It can be made the day before and reheated gently in the oven before serving. It freezes well too.

Serves 8

INGREDIENTS
3 tbsp olive oil
2½ lb boneless leg of lamb, cut into
    1½ in cubes
2 large onions, chopped
2–3 garlic cloves, crushed
2 tbsp flour
1 tsp ground cumin
1 tsp ground coriander
½ tsp ground allspice
3 tbsp tomato paste
1¼ cups lamb stock
⅔ cup red wine
salt and freshly ground black pepper

FOR THE FRUIT PILAF
3 tbsp butter
1 onion, chopped
1 tsp ground turmeric
1¾ cups long grain rice
3⅔ cups stock
⅔ cup dried apricots, chopped
⅔ cup pistachio nuts

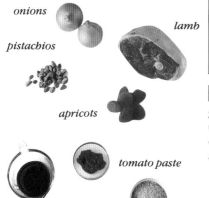

onions

pistachios

apricots

lamb

tomato paste

rice

red wine

1 Preheat the oven to 350°F. Heat the oil in a casserole and brown the meat a few pieces at a time. Remove the lamb after it has browned and keep it warm.

2 Lower the heat, add the onions and garlic to the casserole and cook gently until tender, about 5 minutes, stirring occasionally. Stir in the flour and spices and cook slowly for 3–4 minutes.

3 Stir in the tomato paste, stock and wine, blending them in gradually until the sauce is smooth. Bring to a boil to thicken, and season. Replace the meat, cover the casserole and cook it in the preheated oven for 45–55 minutes, or until the lamb is tender. (Cook for half the time if you are cooking ahead and planning to reheat the next day.)

4 To make the pilaf, melt the butter and cook the onion until tender. Stir in the turmeric and rice and cook for 2 minutes. Then add the stock and season. Bring to a boil, cover and cook in the oven for 20–30 minutes, or until the rice is tender and all the liquid has been absorbed. Stir in the apricots and pistachio nuts, cover and let stand for 10–15 minutes.

Roast Goose with Caramelized Apples and Port and Orange Gravy

Choose a young goose with a pliable breast bone.

Serves 8

INGREDIENTS
10–12 lb goose, with giblets
salt and freshly ground black pepper

FOR THE APPLE AND NUT STUFFING
2 cups prunes
⅔ cup port or red wine
1½ lb cooking apples, peeled, cored
    and cubed
1 large onion, chopped
4 celery stalks, sliced
1 tbsp mixed dried herbs
finely grated rind of 1 orange
goose liver, chopped
1 lb bulk pork sausage
1 cup chopped pecans or
    walnuts
2 eggs

FOR THE CARAMELIZED APPLES
4 tbsp butter
4 tbsp red currant jelly
2 tbsp red wine vinegar
8 small apples, peeled and cored

FOR THE GRAVY
2 tbsp all-purpose flour
2½ cups giblet stock
juice of 1 orange

apples

goose

prunes

orange

onion   eggs

sausage

1 The day before you want to cook the goose, soak the prunes in the port or red wine. Then pit each one and cut it into four pieces, reserving the port.

2 Mix with all the remaining stuffing ingredients and season well. Moisten with half the reserved port.

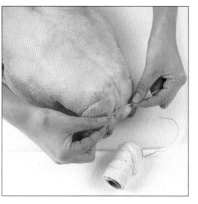

3 Preheat the oven to 400°F. Stuff the neck-end of the goose, tucking the flap of skin under and securing it with a small skewer. Remove the excess fat from the cavity and pack it with the stuffing. Tie the legs together to hold them in place.

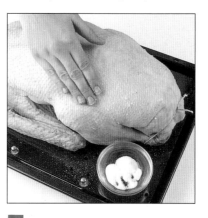

4 Weigh the stuffed goose and calculate the cooking time: allow 15 minutes per 1 lb. Put the bird on a rack in a roasting pan and rub the skin with salt. You may prick the skin all over to help the fat run out. Roast it for 30 minutes, then reduce the heat to 350°F and roast for the remaining cooking time. Pour off any fat produced during cooking into a bowl. The goose is cooked if the juices run clear when the thickest part of the thigh has been pierced with a skewer. Pour a little cold water over the breast to crisp the skin.

5 Meanwhile, prepare the apples. Melt the butter, red currant jelly and vinegar in a small roasting pan or a shallow ovenproof dish. Put in the apples, baste them well and cook in the oven for 15–20 minutes. Baste the apples halfway through the cooking time. Do not overcook them or they will collapse.

6 Place the goose on a serving dish and let it stand for 15 minutes before carving to make the gravy. Pour off the excess fat from the roasting pan, leaving any sediment in the bottom. Stir in the flour, cook gently until golden brown, and then blend in the stock. Bring to a boil, add the remaining reserved port, orange juice and seasoning. Simmer for 2–3 minutes. Strain into a gravy boat. Surround the goose with the caramelized apples and spoon the red currant glaze over.

Tenderloin of Pork Wrapped in Bacon

This easy-to-carve roast is served with an onion and prune gravy.

Serves 8

INGREDIENTS

3 large pork fillets, weighing about
    2½ lb in total
8 oz lean bacon
2 tbsp butter
⅔ cup red wine

FOR THE PRUNE STUFFING
2 tbsp butter
1 onion, very finely chopped
1⅓ cups mushrooms, very finely
    chopped
4 ready-to-eat prunes, pitted and
    chopped
2 tsp dried mixed herbs
2 cups fresh white bread crumbs
1 egg
salt and freshly ground black pepper

TO FINISH
16 ready-to-eat prunes
⅔ cup red wine
16 pickling onions
2 tbsp all-purpose flour
1¼ cups fresh or canned chicken
    stock

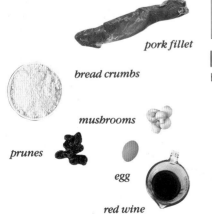

pork fillet

bread crumbs

mushrooms

prunes

egg

red wine

1 Preheat the oven to 350°F. Trim the fillets, removing any sinew and fat. Cut each fillet lengthways, three-quarters of the way through, open them out and flatten.

2 For the stuffing, melt the butter and cook the onion until tender, add the mushrooms and cook for 5 minutes. Transfer to a bowl and mix in the remaining stuffing ingredients. Spread the stuffing over two of the fillets and sandwich together with the third fillet.

3 Stretch each strip of bacon with the back of a large knife.

4 Lay the strips overlapping across the meat. Cut lengths of string and lay them at ¾ in intervals over the bacon. Cover with a piece of foil to hold in place, and roll the tied fillets over. Fold the bacon strips over the meat and tie the string to secure them in place. Roll the fillets back on to the bacon joins and remove the foil.

5 Place in a roasting pan and spread the butter over the pork. Pour around the wine and cook for 1¼ hours, basting occasionally with the liquid in the roasting pan, until evenly browned. Simmer the remaining prunes in the red wine until tender. Boil the onions in salted water for 10 minutes, or until just tender. Drain and add to the prunes.

6 Transfer the pork to a serving plate, remove the string, cover loosely with foil and leave to stand for 10–15 minutes, before slicing. Remove any fat from the roasting pan, add the flour to the sediment and juices and cook gently for 2–3 minutes. Then blend in the stock, bring to a boil and simmer for 5 minutes. Adjust the seasoning to taste. Strain the gravy on to the prunes and onions, reheat and serve in a sauce boat with a ladle.

Individual Beef Wellingtons

The sauce can be made the day before and reheated just before serving. The Wellingtons can be made several hours before cooking, as long as the meat is quite cold before you wrap it in pastry. Keep them in the refrigerator before cooking.

Serves 8

INGREDIENTS
2 tbsp olive oil
8 beef fillet steaks, cut 1 in thick,
    weighing about 4 oz each
2 lb puff pastry, thawed if frozen
8 oz smooth liverwurst or pâté
2 tbsp chopped fresh parsley
2 tbsp chopped fresh chives
1 egg, beaten with 1 tbsp water

FOR THE SAUCE
2 tbsp butter
1 onion, finely chopped
1⅓ cups mushrooms, finely
    chopped
2 tbsp all-purpose flour
½ tsp tomato paste
½ tsp superfine sugar
⅔ cup red wine
1¼ cups beef stock
salt and freshly ground black pepper

1 Heat the oil in a large frying pan and quickly brown the steaks on both sides. Transfer to a plate and leave to cool. Preheat the oven to 400°F.

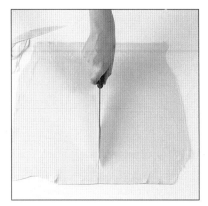

2 Divide the pastry in two equal halves. On a lightly floured work surface, roll each piece out thinly and trim to a 16 in square. Cut into four 8 in squares. (Save the trimmings for the decoration.)

3 Mix the liverwurst or pâté with the herbs. Place a cold filet steak on each piece of pastry and divide the wurst or pâté between each. Spread evenly over the top and sides.

beef stock

puff pastry

butter

fillet steak

liverwurst

tomato paste

red wine

egg

onion

mushrooms

parsley

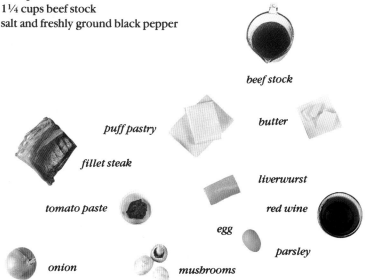

4 Brush the pastry with beaten egg and fold the sides over like a package. Pinch the edges to seal.

5 Place on baking trays, seam-side down and decorate the tops with a lattice cut from the trimmings. When ready to cook them, brush the pastry all over with beaten egg and bake for 25 minutes, or until golden brown. (Do not brush the Wellingtons with egg until just before baking, as the egg dries in the fridge.)

6 To make the sauce, heat the butter and cook the onion until tender. Add the mushrooms and cook for 5 minutes, stirring occasionally. Stir in the flour, tomato paste and sugar and blend in the red wine and stock. Bring to a boil and simmer for 10 minutes. Season to taste, then strain into a gravy boat and serve separately.

Filo Vegetable Pie

This marvelous pie makes a delicious main course for vegetarians or is an excellent accompaniment to cold sliced turkey or other meat dishes.

Serves 6–8

INGREDIENTS
8 oz leeks
11 tbsp butter
8 oz carrots, cubed
8 oz mushrooms, sliced
8 oz Brussels sprouts, quartered
2 garlic cloves, crushed
4 oz cream cheese
4 oz Roquefort or Stilton cheese
⅔ cup heavy cream
2 eggs, beaten
8 oz apples
8 oz/1 cup cashew nuts or pine nuts, toasted
12 oz frozen filo pastry, defrosted
salt and freshly ground black pepper

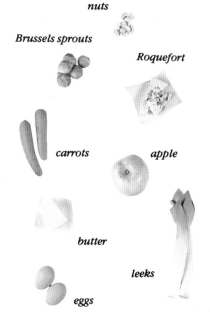

nuts

Brussels sprouts

Roquefort

carrots

apple

butter

leeks

eggs

1 Preheat the oven to 350°F. Cut the leeks in half through the root and wash them to remove any sand, separating the layers slightly to check they are clean. Slice into ½ in pieces, drain and dry on paper towels.

2 Heat 3 tbsp of the butter in a large pan and cook the leeks and carrots, covered, over a medium heat for 5 minutes. Add the mushrooms, sprouts and garlic and cook for another 2 minutes, stirring to coat them with the butter. Turn the vegetables into a bowl and let them cool.

3 Whisk the cream cheese and blue cheese, cream, eggs and seasoning together in a bowl. Pour them over the vegetables. Peel and core the apples and cut into ½ in cubes. Add them to the vegetables, with the toasted nuts.

4 Melt the remaining butter. Brush the inside of a 9 in loose-based springform cake pan with melted butter. Brush two-thirds of the filo pastry sheets with butter one at a time, and use them to line the base and sides of the pan, overlapping the layers so that there are no gaps.

5 Spoon in the vegetable mixture and fold over the excess filo pastry to cover the filling.

6 Brush the remaining filo sheets with butter and cut them into 1 in strips. Cover the top of the pie with these strips, arranging them in a rough mound. Bake for 35–45 minutes until golden brown all over. Allow to stand for 5 minutes, and then remove the cake pan and transfer to a serving plate.

Cheese and Spinach Quiche

This quiche freezes well and can be reheated. It's an excellent addition to a festive buffet party and is popular with vegetarians too. If you don't have a lattice cutter, cut the pastry into strips and make a lattice following the instructions given for the Deluxe Mincemeat Tart.

Serves 8

INGREDIENTS
½ cup butter
2 cups all-purpose flour
½ tsp English mustard powder
½ tsp paprika
large pinch of salt
4 oz Cheddar cheese, finely grated
3–4 tbsp cold water
1 egg, beaten, to glaze

FOR THE FILLING
1 lb frozen spinach
1 onion, chopped
pinch of grated nutmeg
8 oz cottage cheese
2 large eggs
2 oz Parmesan cheese, grated
⅔ cup light cream
salt and freshly ground black pepper

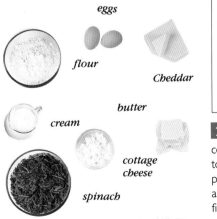

eggs
flour
Cheddar
butter
cream
cottage cheese
spinach

1 Rub the butter into the flour until it resembles fine bread crumbs. Rub in the next four ingredients. Bind to a dough with the cold water. Knead until smooth, wrap and chill for 30 minutes.

2 Put the spinach and onion in a pan, cover, and cook slowly. Increase the heat to evaporate any water. Season with salt, pepper and nutmeg. Turn the spinach into a bowl, cool slightly. Add the remaining filling ingredients.

3 Preheat the oven to 400°F. Put a baking tray in the oven to preheat. Cut one-third off the pastry for the lid. On a lightly floured surface, roll out the remaining pastry and use it to line a 9 in loose-based cake pan. Press the pastry well into the edges and make a narrow lip around the top edge. Remove the excess pastry with a rolling pin. Pour the filling into the pie crust.

4 Roll out the remaining pastry and cut it with a lattice pastry cutter. Carefully open the lattice. With the help of a rolling pin, lay it over the quiche. Brush the joins with egg glaze. Press the edges together and trim off the excess pastry. Brush the pastry lattice with egg glaze and bake on the hot baking tray for 35–40 minutes, or until golden brown. Serve hot or cold.

Gratin Dauphinois

This dish can be made and baked in advance; reheat it in the oven for 20–30 minutes. This is a good alternative to roast potatoes and it needs no last-minute attention.

Serves 8

INGREDIENTS
butter, for greasing
3½ lb potatoes
2–3 garlic cloves, crushed
½ tsp grated nutmeg
4 oz Cheddar cheese, grated
2½ cups milk
1¼ cups light cream
2 large eggs, beaten
salt and freshly ground black pepper

cream

potatoes

Cheddar

eggs

nutmeg

garlic

1 Preheat the oven to 350°F. Butter a 10 cup shallow ovenproof dish. Scrub and peel the potatoes and slice them thinly.

2 Layer the potatoes in the dish, with the garlic, nutmeg and two-thirds of the grated cheese and season well.

3 Whisk the milk, cream and eggs together and pour them over the potatoes, making sure the liquid goes all the way to the bottom of the dish.

4 Scatter the remaining cheese on top and bake for 45–50 minutes, or until golden brown. Test the potatoes with a sharp knife; they should be very tender.

Cheese, Rice and Vegetable Strudel

Based on a traditional Russian dish called 'Koulibiac', this makes a perfect vegetarian main course or an unusual accompaniment to cold leftover turkey or sliced ham.

Serves 8

INGREDIENTS
⅞ cup long grain rice
2 tbsp butter
1–2 leeks, thinly sliced
12 oz mushrooms, sliced
8 oz Gruyère or Cheddar cheese, grated
8 oz feta cheese, cubed
2 tbsp raisins
½ cup chopped almonds or hazelnuts, toasted
2 tbsp chopped fresh parsley
10 oz package frozen filo pastry, thawed
2 tbsp olive oil
salt and freshly ground black pepper

feta

leek

rice

parsley

filo pastry

almonds

mushrooms

raisins

1 Cook the rice in boiling, salted water for 10–12 minutes, until tender. Drain, rinse under cold running water and set aside. Melt the butter and cook the leeks and mushrooms for 5 minutes. Transfer to a bowl to cool.

2 Add the well-drained rice, the cheeses, raisins, toasted nuts, parsley and season to taste (be careful with the salt as the feta cheese is very salty).

3 Preheat the oven to 375°F. Unwrap the filo pastry. Cover it with a piece of plastic wrap and a damp cloth while you work. Lay a sheet of filo pastry on a large piece of wax paper and brush it with oil. Lay a second sheet, overlapping the first by 1 in. Put another sheet with its long side running at right angles to the long sides of the first two. Lay a fourth sheet in the same way, overlapping by 1 in. Continue in this way, alternating the layers of two sheets so that the join between the two sheets runs in the opposite direction for each layer.

4 Place the filling along the center of the pastry and shape it neatly with your hands into a rectangle approximately 4 × 12 in.

5 Fold the pastry over the filling and roll it over, with the help of the wax paper, so that the join is hidden underneath.

6 Lift the strudel on to a greased baking tray and tuck the edges under, so that the filling does not escape during cooking. Brush with oil and bake for 30–40 minutes, until golden and crisp. Let the strudel stand for 5 minutes before cutting.

Vegetable Cheese Puff

This makes a light vegetarian supper, or a main meal served with a salad and baked potatoes.

Serves 4

INGREDIENTS
4 tbsp butter
2/3 cup water
2/3 cup all-purpose flour
2 eggs, beaten
1/4 tsp English mustard
2 oz Cheddar or Gruyère cheese,
   cubed
salt and freshly ground black pepper
2 tsp chopped fresh parsley,
   to garnish

FOR THE FILLING
2 tbsp butter
1 onion, sliced
1 garlic clove, crushed
2 2/3 cups mushrooms, sliced
1 tbsp all-purpose flour
1 × 14 oz can tomatoes
1 tsp superfine sugar
8 oz zucchini, sliced thickly

FOR THE TOPPING
1 tbsp grated Parmesan cheese
1 tbsp bread crumbs, toasted

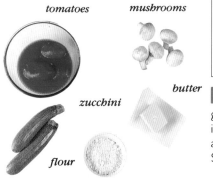

tomatoes   *mushrooms*   *butter*   *zucchini*   *flour*

1 Preheat the oven to 400°F. To make the choux pastry, melt the butter in a pan, add the water and bring to a boil. As soon as the liquid is boiling, draw the pan off the heat and beat in the flour all at once, until a smooth paste is formed. Turn into a large bowl and allow to cool slightly.

2 With an electric whisk, beat the eggs gradually into the paste until the mixture is glossy but firm. Season with salt, pepper and mustard powder. Fold in the cheese. Set aside.

3 To make the filling, melt the butter in a pan and cook the onion gently until tender. Add the garlic and mushrooms and cook for 2–3 minutes. Stir in the flour and the tomatoes and their juice. Bring to the boil, stirring, to thicken. Season with salt, pepper and sugar to taste. Lastly add the sliced zucchini.

4 Butter a 5 cup ovenproof dish. Spoon the choux pastry in rough mounds around the sides of the dish and turn the filling into the center. Sprinkle the Parmesan cheese and bread crumbs on top of the filling. Bake for 35–40 minutes, until the pastry is well risen and golden brown. Sprinkle with chopped parsley and serve hot.

Vegetable Crumble with Anchovies

The anchovies may be left out of this dish in order that vegetarians can enjoy it, but they give the vegetables a delicious flavor. Serve as an accompaniment to sliced turkey or ham.

Serves 8

INGREDIENTS
1 lb potatoes
8 oz leeks
2 tbsp butter
1 lb carrots, chopped
2 garlic cloves, crushed
2⅓ cups mushrooms, sliced
1 lb Brussels sprouts, sliced
1 × 1½ oz can anchovies, drained
salt and freshly ground black pepper

FOR THE CHEESE CRUMBLE
4 tbsp all-purpose flour
4 tbsp butter
1 cup fresh bread crumbs
2 oz Cheddar cheese, grated
2 tbsp chopped fresh parsley
1 tsp English mustard powder

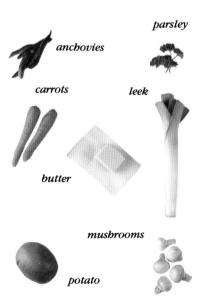

anchovies

parsley

carrots

leek

butter

mushrooms

potato

1 Peel and halve the potatoes and parboil them in salted water until just tender. Drain and cool. Cut the leeks in half lengthwise and wash them thoroughly to remove any sand. Drain and slice in ½ in pieces.

2 Melt the butter and cook the leeks and carrots for 2–3 minutes. Add the garlic and mushrooms and cook for a further 3 minutes. Add the sprouts. Season with pepper. Transfer to a 10 cup ovenproof dish.

3 Preheat the oven to 400°F. Chop the anchovies and scatter them over the vegetables. Slice the potatoes and arrange them on top.

4 To make the crumble, sift the flour into a bowl and rub in the butter or process in a food processor. Add the bread crumbs and mix in the remaining ingredients. Spoon over the vegetables and bake for 20–30 minutes.

Vegetable Gnocchi

This delicious vegetarian main course can be assembled well ahead of time and cooked in the oven without any last-minute preparation.

Serves 8

INGREDIENTS
1 lb frozen spinach
1 tbsp butter
¼ tsp grated nutmeg
8 oz ricotta or farmer's cheese
4 oz Parmesan cheese, grated
2 eggs, beaten
1 cup all-purpose flour
2 oz Cheddar cheese, grated
salt and freshly ground black pepper

FOR THE SAUCE
4 tbsp butter
4 tbsp all-purpose flour
2½ cups milk

FOR THE VEGETABLE LAYER
2 tbsp butter
2 leeks or onions, sliced
4 carrots, sliced
4 celery stalks, sliced
4 zucchini, sliced

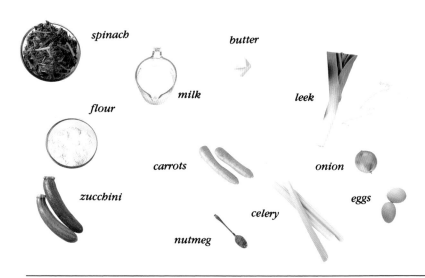

spinach
butter
milk
flour
leek
carrots
onion
zucchini
eggs
celery
nutmeg

1 Put the spinach in a large pan with the butter and heat gently to defrost it. Then increase the heat to drive off any moisture. Season with salt, pepper and nutmeg. Turn into a bowl and mix in the ricotta or farmer's cheese, Parmesan cheese, eggs and flour. Beat until smooth.

2 Shape the mixture into ovals with two dessertspoons and place them on a lightly floured tray. Place in the refrigerator for 30 minutes.

3 Have a large shallow pan of boiling, salted water ready. Cook the gnocchi in two batches, for about 5 minutes (the water should simmer gently and not boil). As soon as the gnocchi rise to the surface, remove them with a slotted spoon and let them drain on a clean dish towel.

4 Preheat the oven to 350°F. For the sauce, melt the butter in a pan, add the flour and blend in the milk. Bring to a boil to thicken and season to taste.

5 For the vegetable layer, melt the butter and cook the leeks, carrots and celery until tender, about 5 minutes. Add the zucchini, season with salt and pepper and stir to mix. Turn into a 10 cup ovenproof dish.

6 Place the drained gnocchi on top, spoon over the sauce and sprinkle with grated cheese. Bake for 30 minutes, until golden brown. Broil if necessary.

Brussels Sprouts with Chestnut and Carrots

Be sure to allow plenty of time to peel the chestnuts; it is fussy work but well worth the effort.

Serves 8

INGREDIENTS
1 lb fresh chestnuts
1⅞ cups vegetable stock
1 lb Brussels sprouts
1 lb carrots
2 tbsp butter
salt and freshly ground black pepper

carrots

butter

chestnuts

Brussels sprouts

1 Using a sharp knife, peel the raw chestnuts, leaving the brown papery skins intact. Bring a small pan of water to a boil, drop a handful of chestnuts into the water for a few minutes, and remove with a slotted spoon. The brown papery skins will slip off easily.

2 Put the peeled chestnuts in a pan with the stock. Cover the pan and bring to a boil. Simmer for 5–10 minutes, until tender. Drain.

3 Remove the outer leaves from the sprouts, if necessary, and trim the stalks level. Cook in a pan of boiling, salted water for about 5 minutes, or until just tender. Drain and rinse under cold running water to stop the cooking.

4 Peel the carrots and cut them in ½ in diagonal slices. Put them in a pan with cold water to cover, bring to a boil and simmer until just tender, 5–6 minutes. Drain and rinse under cold running water. Melt the butter in a heavy-based pan, add the chestnuts, sprouts and carrots and season with salt and pepper. Cover with a lid and reheat, occasionally stirring the vegetables in the pan.

Sweet and Sour Red Cabbage

The cabbage can be cooked the day before and reheated for serving. It is a good accompaniment to goose, pork or strong-flavored game dishes. The crispy bacon added at the end of cooking is optional and can be omitted.

Serves 8

INGREDIENTS

2 lb red cabbage
2 tbsp olive oil
2 large onions, sliced
2 large apples, peeled, cored and
    sliced
2 tbsp cider vinegar
2 tbsp brown sugar
8 oz lean bacon (optional)
salt and freshly ground black pepper

apples

olive oil

cider vinegar

cabbage

brown sugar

bacon *onions*

1 Preheat the oven to 350°F. Cut the cabbage into quarters through the stalk and shred it finely with a sharp knife or in a food processor, discarding the hard core.

2 Heat the oil in a large ovenproof casserole. Cook the onion over a gentle heat for 2 minutes.

3 Stir the cabbage, apples, vinegar, sugar and seasoning into the casserole. Cover with a tight-fitting lid and cook for about 1 hour, or until very tender. Stir halfway through cooking.

4 Chop the bacon, if using, and fry it gently in a pan until crisp. Stir it into the cabbage just before serving.

Vegetarian Christmas Torte

A sophisticated mushroom torte with a cheese-soufflé topping. Serve hot with cranberry relish and Brussels Sprouts with Chestnuts and Carrots.

Serves 8

INGREDIENTS
2 cups all-purpose flour
¾ cup butter
2 tsp paprika
4 oz Parmesan cheese, grated
1 egg, beaten with 1 tbsp cold water
1 tbsp Dijon mustard

FOR THE FILLING
2 tbsp butter
1 onion, finely chopped
1–2 garlic cloves, crushed
12 oz mushrooms, chopped
2 tsp dried mixed herbs
1 tbsp chopped fresh parsley
1 cup fresh white bread crumbs
salt and freshly ground black pepper

FOR THE CHEESE TOPPING
2 tbsp butter
2 tbsp all-purpose flour
1¼ cups milk
1 oz Parmesan cheese, grated
3 oz Cheddar cheese, grated
¼ tsp English mustard powder
1 egg, separated

1 To make the pastry, sift the flour into a bowl and rub in the butter until the mixture resembles fine bread crumbs. Stir in the paprika and Parmesan cheese. Bind to a soft pliable dough with the egg and water. Knead until smooth, wrap in plastic wrap and chill for 30 minutes.

2 For the filling, melt the butter and cook the onion until tender. Add the garlic and mushrooms and cook, uncovered, for 5 minutes, stirring occasionally. Increase the heat and drive off any liquid in the pan. Remove the pan from the heat and stir in the dried herbs, parsley, bread crumbs and seasoning. Allow to cool.

3 Preheat the oven to 375°F. Put a baking sheet in the oven. On a lightly floured surface, roll out the pastry and use it to line a 9 in loose-based cake pan, pressing the pastry well into the edges and making a narrow rim around the top edge. Chill for 20 minutes.

4 For the cheese topping, melt the butter in a pan, stir in the flour and cook for 2 minutes. Gradually blend in the milk. Bring to a boil to thicken and simmer for 2–3 minutes. Remove the pan from the heat and stir in the cheeses, mustard powder and egg yolk, and season well. Beat until smooth. Whisk the egg white until it holds soft peaks; fold the egg white into the topping.

cheese

butter

flour

parsley

onion

garlic

bread crumbs

mushrooms

5 To assemble the torte, spread the Dijon mustard evenly over the base of the crust. Spoon in the mushroom filling and level the surface.

6 Pour over the cheese topping and bake the torte on the hot baking tray for 35–45 minutes until set and golden.

Game Terrine

Any game can be used to make this country terrine.
The ovenproof dish that it is cooked in must have a lid,
to seal in all the flavors during the long cooking time.

Serves 8

INGREDIENTS
8 oz lean bacon
8 oz lamb or pork liver, ground
1 lb ground pork
1 small onion, finely chopped
2 garlic cloves, crushed
2 tsp dried mixed herbs
8 oz game (e.g., hare, rabbit, or
    pheasant)
4 tbsp port or sherry
1 bay leaf
½ cup all-purpose flour
1¼ cups jelly stock, made with beef
    stock and gelatin
salt and freshly ground black pepper

bacon

port

herbs

ground pork

liver

bay leaf

onion

1 Remove the rind from the bacon and stretch each strip with the back of a heavy knife. Use the rindless bacon strips to line a 4 cup terrine.

2 In a bowl, mix together the ground pork and liver with the onion, garlic and dried herbs. Season with salt and pepper.

3 Cut the game into thin strips and put it into a bowl with the port or sherry. Season with salt and pepper and leave to marinate for 1 hour.

4 Put one-third of the ground mixture into the terrine, pressing it well into the corners. Cover with half the strips of game and repeat these layers, ending with a ground layer. Level the surface and lay the bay leaf on top.

5 Preheat the oven to 325°F. Put the flour into a small bowl and mix it to a firm dough with 2–3 tbsp cold water. Cover the terrine with a lid and seal it with the flour paste. Place the terrine in a roasting pan and pour enough hot water around to come halfway up the sides of the dish. Cook in the oven for 2 hours.

6 Remove the lid and weight the terrine down with a 4 lb weight. Leave to cool. Remove any fat from the surface and cover with warmed jelly stock. Let set overnight before turning out.

Turkey and Cranberry Pie

The cranberries add a tart layer to this turkey pie. Cranberry sauce can be used if fresh cranberries are not available. The pie freezes well.

Serves 8

INGREDIENTS
1 lb bulk pork sausage
1 lb lean ground pork
1 tbsp ground coriander
1 tbsp dried mixed herbs
finely grated rind of 2 large oranges
2 tsp grated fresh ginger root or ½ tsp ground ginger
2 tsp salt
1 lb turkey breast fillets, thinly sliced
4 oz fresh cranberries
freshly ground black pepper

FOR THE PASTRY
4 cups all-purpose flour
1 tsp salt
⅔ cup shortening
⅔ cup mixed milk and water

TO FINISH
1 egg, beaten
1¼ cups jelly stock, made with chicken stock and gelatin

cranberries   turkey fillets

pork

ginger   herbs

orange   coriander

1 Preheat the oven to 350°F. Place a baking sheet in the oven to preheat. In a bowl, mix together the sausage, pork, coriander, herbs, orange rind, ginger and salt and pepper.

2 To make the pastry, put the flour into a large bowl with the salt. Heat the shortening in a small pan with the milk and water until just beginning to boil. Take the pan off the heat and let cool slightly.

3 Using a wooden spoon, quickly stir the liquid into the flour until a very stiff dough is formed. Turn on to a work surface and knead until smooth. Cut one-third off the dough for the lid, wrap it in plastic wrap and keep it in a warm place.

4 Roll out the large piece of dough on a floured surface and line the base and sides of a well-greased 8 in loose-based, springform cake pan. Work with the dough while it is still warm, as it will crack and break if it is left to get cold.

5 Put the turkey pieces between two pieces of plastic wrap and flatten with a rolling pin to a thickness of 1/8 in. Spoon half the pork mixture into the base of the pan, pressing it well into the edges. Cover with half of the turkey slices and then the cranberries, followed by the remaining turkey and finally the rest of the pork mixture.

6 Roll out the rest of the dough and cover the filling, trimming any excess and sealing the edges with a little beaten egg. Make a steam hole in the center of the lid and decorate the top by cutting pastry trimmings into leaf shapes. Brush with beaten egg. Bake for 2 hours. Cover the pie with foil if the top gets too brown. Place the pie on a wire rack to cool. When cold, use a funnel to fill the pie with liquid jelly stock. Let set for a few hours or overnight, before unmolding the pie to serve it.

Turkey Rice Salad

A delicious, crunchy salad to use up leftover turkey during the holiday festivities.

Serves 8

INGREDIENTS
1¼ cups brown rice
⅔ cup wild rice
2 red apples, quartered, cored and
  chopped
2 celery stalks, coarsely sliced
4 oz seedless grapes
3 tbsp lemon or orange juice
⅔ cup thick mayonnaise, homemade
  or store bought
12 oz cooked turkey, chopped
salt and freshly ground black pepper
frilly lettuce leaves, to serve

lettuce leaves

celery

mayonnaise

turkey

brown rice

grapes

wild rice

apples

1 Cook the brown and wild rice together in plenty of boiling salted water for 25 minutes, or until tender. Rinse under cold running water and drain thoroughly.

2 Turn into a large bowl and add the apples, celery and grapes. Beat the lemon or orange juice into the mayonnaise, season with salt and pepper and pour over the rice.

3 Add the turkey and mix well to coat with the lemon or orange mayonnaise.

4 Arrange the frilly lettuce over the base and around the sides of a serving dish and spoon the rice on top.

Ham and Bulgur Wheat Salad

This unusual, nutty salad uses up leftover cooked ham for a quick meal on New Year's Day.

Serves 8

INGREDIENTS
8 oz bulgur wheat
3 tbsp olive oil
2 tbsp lemon juice
1 red bell pepper
8 oz cooked ham, diced
2 tbsp chopped fresh mint
2 tbsp raisins
salt and freshly ground black pepper
sprigs of fresh mint and lemon slices,
    to garnish

bulgur wheat

olive oil

mint

ham

currants

red pepper

lemon

1 Put the bulgur wheat into a bowl, pour over enough boiling water to cover and leave to stand until all the water has been absorbed.

2 Add the oil, lemon juice, and seasoning to taste. Toss to separate the grains using two forks.

3 Quarter the pepper, removing the stalk and seeds. Cut it into wide strips and then into diamonds. Add the pepper, ham, mint and currants. Transfer to a serving dish and garnish with sprigs of fresh mint and lemon slices.

COOK'S TIP

This salad can also be made with 8 oz couscous instead of the bulgur wheat. Cover the couscous with boiling water as in step 1.

Layered Salmon Terrine

This elegant fish mousse is perfect for a buffet table or first course. Slice with a sharp knife.

Serves 8

INGREDIENTS
⅞ cup milk
4 tbsp butter
⅔ cup all-purpose flour
1 lb fresh haddock fillet, boned and skinned
12 oz fresh salmon fillet, boned and skinned
2 eggs, beaten
4 tbsp heavy cream
4 oz smoked salmon or trout, cut in strips
salt and freshly ground black pepper

1 Heat the milk and butter in a saucepan until the milk is boiling, take the pan off the heat and beat in the flour until a thick smooth paste forms. Season with salt and pepper, turn out on to a plate and let cool.

2 Put the haddock into a food processor and process it until smooth. Put it into a bowl. Process the salmon fillet in the same way and put it into a separate bowl. Add an egg and half the cream to each of the fish mixtures. Beat in half the milk and flour paste to each mixture.

3 Preheat the oven to 350°F. Butter a 2 lb loaf pan and line it with a piece of wax paper. Lay strips of smoked salmon or trout diagonally over the base and up the sides of the lined pan.

haddock

cream

flour

butter

fresh salmon

milk

eggs

smoked salmon

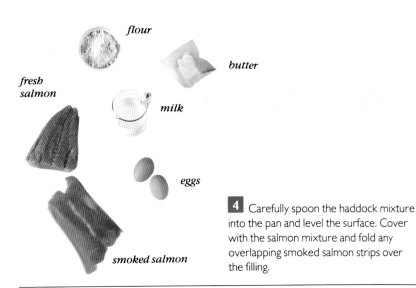

4 Carefully spoon the haddock mixture into the pan and level the surface. Cover with the salmon mixture and fold any overlapping smoked salmon strips over the filling.

5 Cover the loaf pan with a piece of buttered wax paper and then a layer of foil. Place it in a roasting pan and pour enough hot water around to come halfway up the sides of the pan. Cook for 40 minutes, or until firm to the touch.

6 Remove from the oven and stand for 10 minutes. Turn the terrine out on to a serving plate and serve it warm or let cool.

Fillet of Beef with Ratatouille

This succulent rare beef is served cold with a colorful garlicky ratatouille.

Serves 8

INGREDIENTS
1½–2 lb fillet of beef
3 tbsp olive oil
1¼ cups jelly stock, made with beef stock and gelatin

FOR THE MARINADE
2 tbsp sherry
2 tbsp olive oil
2 tbsp soy sauce
2 tsp grated fresh ginger root or 1 tsp ground ginger
2 garlic cloves, crushed

FOR THE RATATOUILLE
4 tbsp olive oil
1 onion, sliced
2–3 garlic cloves, crushed
1 large eggplant, cubed
1 small red bell pepper, seeded and sliced
1 small green bell pepper, seeded and sliced
1 small yellow bell pepper, seeded and sliced
8 oz zucchini, sliced
1 lb tomatoes, skinned and quartered
1 tbsp chopped fresh mixed herbs
2 tbsp French dressing
salt and freshly ground black pepper

eggplant

tomatoes

peppers

beef

olive oil

ginger

soy sauce

zucchini

onion

sherry

1 Mix all the marinade ingredients together in a shallow dish, put the beef in and turn it over to coat it. Cover with plastic wrap and leave for 30 minutes, to allow the flavors to penetrate the meat.

2 Preheat the oven to 425°F. Lift the fillet out of the marinade and pat it dry with paper towels. Heat the oil in a frying-pan until smoking hot and then brown the beef all over to seal it. Transfer to a roasting pan and roast for 10–15 minutes, basting it with the marinade. Lift the beef on to a plate and let it cool.

3 Meanwhile, for the ratatouille, heat the oil in a large casserole and cook the onion and garlic over a low heat until tender. Add the eggplant and cook for a further 5 minutes, until soft. Add the sliced peppers and zucchini and cook for 2 minutes. Then add the tomatoes, herbs and seasoning and cook for a few minutes longer.

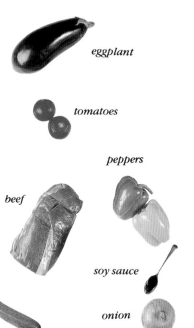

4 Turn the ratatouille into a dish and cool. Drizzle with a little French dressing. Slice the beef and arrange overlapping slices on a serving platter. Brush the slices with cold jelly stock which is on the point of setting.

5 Leave the jelly to set completely, then brush with a second coat. Spoon the ratatouille on to the dish and serve.

Salmon and Pea Ring

A stunning pea and fish mousse with salmon chunks set in it. Serve it hot or cold as a starter, with a delicious herb and lemon sauce.

Serves 8

INGREDIENTS
1 lb fresh haddock, filleted, skinned and cubed
4 oz frozen peas, cooked and cooled
2 eggs
4 tbsp heavy cream
1 lb fresh salmon, filleted, skinned and cubed
salt and freshly ground black pepper
small bunch watercress, to garnish

FOR THE HERB AND LEMON SAUCE
⅔ cup fish stock
8 oz low-fat cream cheese
1 tbsp lemon juice
1 tbsp chopped fresh parsley
1 tbsp chopped fresh chives

1 Check the fish for any stray bones. Preheat the oven to 350°F. Put the haddock and cooked peas into a food processor and process them until smooth.

2 Add the eggs, cream and seasoning to the food processor and mix together thoroughly.

3 Transfer to a bowl and fold in the cubed salmon pieces. Butter a 1¾ pint/4 cup ring mold and spoon in the fish mixture. Level the top and cover it with buttered paper and foil. Put the ring mold into a roasting pan and pour hot water around to come halfway up the sides of the pan. Poach in the oven for 40 minutes, or until the ring is firm to the touch.

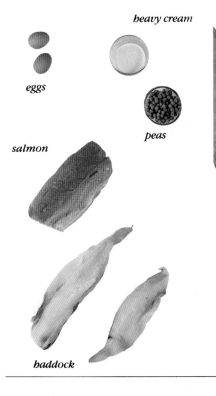

heavy cream

eggs

peas

salmon

haddock

4 Meanwhile, make the sauce. Put the fish stock and cream cheese in a pan and heat gently to melt. Whisk until smooth. Add the lemon juice and herbs and season to taste. Turn the fish mould out on to a serving plate and garnish it with a bunch of watercress in the center. Serve it warm or cold, with the sauce.

Chocolate and Chestnut Yule Log

This is based on the French Bûche de Noël, traditionally served at Christmas. Make it some time in advance and freeze it. It's an excellent dessert for a party.

Serves 8

INGREDIENTS
¼ cup all-purpose flour
2 tbsp cocoa powder
pinch of salt
3 large eggs, separated
large pinch of cream of tartar
8 tbsp superfine sugar
2–3 drops almond extract
sifted cocoa powder and holly sprigs,
   to decorate

FOR THE FILLING
1 tbsp rum or brandy
1 tsp powdered gelatin
4 oz dark chocolate, broken into
   squares
4 tbsp superfine sugar
8 oz canned chestnut purée
1¼ cups heavy cream

1 Preheat the oven to 350°F. Grease and line a 9 × 13 in jelly roll pan and line the base with non-stick baking paper. Sift the flour, cocoa and salt together on to a piece of wax paper.

2 Put the egg whites into a large clean bowl and whisk them until frothy. Add the cream of tartar and whisk until stiff. Gradually whisk in half the sugar, until the mixture will stand in stiff peaks.

3 Put the egg yolks and the remaining sugar into another bowl and whisk until thick and pale. Add the almond extract. Stir in the sifted flour and cocoa mixture. Lastly, fold in the egg whites, using a metal spoon, until everything is evenly blended. Be careful not to overmix.

4 Turn the batter into the prepared jelly roll pan and level the top. Bake for 15–20 minutes, or until springy to the touch. Have ready a large piece of wax paper dusted liberally with superfine sugar. Turn the jelly roll on to the paper, remove the lining paper, and roll it up with the wax paper still inside. Let cool completely on a wire rack.

chestnut purée

flour

cream of tartar

cocoa powder

brandy

cream

eggs

almond extract

dark chocolate

5 Put the brandy in a cup and sprinkle the gelatin over; leave to become spongy. Melt the chocolate in a 2½ cup bowl over a pan of hot water. Melt the gelatin over hot water and add to the chocolate. With an electric beater, whisk in the sugar and chestnut purée. Remove from the heat and let cool. Whisk the cream until it holds soft peaks. Fold the two mixtures together evenly.

6 Unroll the cake carefully, spread it with half the filling and roll it up again. Place it on a serving dish and spread over the rest of the chocolate cream to cover it. Mark it with a fork to resemble a log. Chill until firm. Dust the cake with sifted cocoa powder and decorate the plate with sprigs of holly.

Ginger Trifle

This is a good way to use up leftover cake, whether plain, chocolate or gingerbread. You can substitute honey for the ginger and syrup, if you prefer. This pudding can be made the day before.

Serves 8

INGREDIENTS
8 oz gingerbread or other cake
4 tbsp Grand Marnier or sweet sherry
2 ripe pears, peeled, cored
   and cubed
2 bananas, thickly sliced
2 oranges, segmented
1–2 pieces preserved ginger, finely
   chopped, plus 2 tbsp syrup

FOR THE CUSTARD
2 eggs
4 tbsp superfine sugar
1 tbsp cornstarch
1⅞ cups milk
few drops vanilla extract

TO DECORATE
⅔ cup heavy cream, lightly whipped
¼ cup chopped almonds, toasted
4 candied cherries
8 small pieces angelica

gingerbread
bananas
pear
orange
eggs
candied cherries

1 Cut the gingerbread into 1½ in cubes. Put them in the bottom of a 3 pint/7½ cup glass bowl. Sprinkle the Grand Marnier or sherry over and let soak in.

2 To make the custard, whisk the eggs, sugar and cornstarch together in a bowl with a little of the milk. Heat the remaining milk until it is almost boiling. Pour it on to the egg mixture, whisking all the time. Return to the pan and stir over the heat until thickened. Simmer for 2 minutes, to cook the cornstarch. Add the vanilla extract and let cool.

3 Mix all the prepared fruit with the finely chopped preserved ginger and syrup. Spoon into the bowl on top of the gingerbread. Spoon over the custard to cover and chill until set.

4 Cover the top with whipped cream and sprinkle on the toasted almonds. Arrange the candied cherries and angelica around the edge.

Ruby Fruit Salad

After a rich main course, this port-flavored fruit salad is light and refreshing. Use any fruit that is available.

Serves 8

INGREDIENTS
1¼ cups water
8 tbsp superfine sugar
1 cinnamon stick
4 cloves
pared rind of 1 orange
1¼ cups port
2 oranges
1 small ripe cantaloupe or honeydew
   melon
4 small bananas
2 apples
8 oz seedless grapes

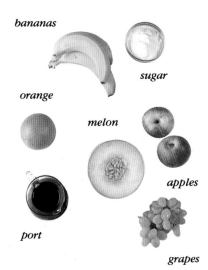

bananas

sugar

orange

melon

apples

port

grapes

1 Put the water, sugar, spices and pared orange rind into a pan and stir over a gentle heat to dissolve the sugar. Then bring to a boil, cover with a lid and simmer for 10 minutes. Let cool, then add the port.

2 Strain the liquid (to remove the spices and orange rind) into a bowl. With a sharp knife, cut off all the skin and pith from the oranges. Then, holding each orange over the bowl to catch the juice, cut away the segments, by slicing between the membrane that divides each segment and allowing the segments to drop into the syrup. Squeeze the remaining pith to release any juice.

3 Cut the melon in half, remove the seeds and scoop out the flesh with a melon baller, or cut it in small cubes. Add it to the syrup.

4 Peel the bananas and cut them diagonally in ½ in slices. Quarter and core the apples and cut them in small cubes. Leave the skin on, or peel them if it is tough. Halve the grapes if large or leave them whole. Stir all the fruit into the syrup, cover with plastic wrap and chill for an hour before serving.

Christmas Pudding

This recipe makes enough to fill one 5 cup mold or two 2½ cup molds. It can be made up to a month before Christmas and stored in a cool, dry place. Steam the pudding for 2 hours before serving. Serve with brandy or rum butter, whisky sauce, custard or whipped cream, topped with a decorative sprig of holly.

Serves 8

INGREDIENTS
½ cup butter
1 heaped cup soft dark brown sugar
½ cup self-rising flour
1 tsp ground allspice
¼ tsp grated nutmeg
½ tsp ground cinnamon
2 eggs
2 cups fresh white bread crumbs
1 cup sultanas
1 cup raisins
½ cup currants
3 tbsp mixed candied citrus peel, chopped finely
¼ cup chopped almonds
1 small apple, peeled, cored and coarsely grated
finely grated rind of 1 orange or lemon
juice of 1 orange or lemon, made up to ⅔ cup with brandy, rum or sherry

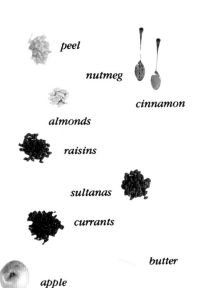

peel

nutmeg

cinnamon

almonds

bread crumbs

raisins

sultanas

currants

brown sugar

orange

butter

apple

1 Cut a disc of wax paper to fit the base of the mold(s) and butter the disc and mold(s).

2 Whisk the butter and sugar together until soft. Beat in the flour, spices and eggs. Stir in the remaining ingredients thoroughly. The mixture should have a soft dropping consistency.

3 Turn the mixture into the greased mold(s) and level the top.

4 Cover with another disc of buttered wax paper.

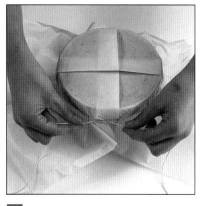

5 Make a pleat across the center of a large piece of wax paper and cover the mold(s) with it, tying it in place with string under the rim. Cut off the excess paper. Pleat a piece of foil in the same way and cover the mold(s) with it, tucking it around the bowl neatly, under the wax frill. Tie another piece of string around the mold(s) and across the top, as a handle.

6 Place the mold(s) in a steamer over a pan of simmering water and steam for 6 hours. Alternatively, put the mold(s) into a large pan and pour enough boiling water around to come halfway up the mold(s) and cover the pan with a tight-fitting lid. Check the water is simmering and top it up with boiling water as it evaporates. When the pudding(s) have cooked, let cool completely. Then remove the foil and wax paper. Wipe the mold(s) clean and replace the wax paper and foil with clean pieces, ready for reheating.

TO SERVE

Steam for 2 hours. Turn on to a plate and let stand for 5 minutes, before removing the pudding mold (the steam will rise to the top of the mold and help to loosen the pudding).

De Luxe Mincemeat Tart

The mincemeat can be made up and kept in the fridge for up to two weeks. It can also be used to make individual mince pies.

Serves 8

INGREDIENTS

2 cups all-purpose flour
2 tsp ground cinnamon
⅔ cup walnuts, finely ground
½ cup butter
4 tbsp superfine sugar, plus extra for
  dusting
1 egg
2 drops vanilla extract
1 tbsp cold water

FOR THE MINCEMEAT

2 apples, peeled, cored and coarsely
  grated
1⅓ cups raisins
⅔ cup ready-to-eat dried apricots,
  chopped
⅔ cup ready-to-eat dried figs or
  prunes, chopped
8 oz green grapes, halved and seeded
½ cup chopped almonds
finely grated rind of 1 lemon
2 tbsp lemon juice
2 tbsp brandy or port
¼ tsp ground allspice
generous ½ cup light brown sugar
2 tbsp butter, melted

brandy

brown sugar

walnuts

raisins

apple

apricots

almonds

grapes

port

lemon

butter

figs

1 To make the pastry, put the flour, cinnamon and walnuts in a food processor. Add the butter and process until the mixture resembles fine bread crumbs. Turn into a bowl and stir in the sugar. Using a fork, beat the egg with the vanilla extract and water. Gradually stir the egg mixture into the dry ingredients. Gather together with your fingertips to form a soft, pliable dough. Knead briefly on a lightly floured surface until smooth; then wrap the dough in plastic wrap and chill it for 30 minutes.

2 Mix all the mincemeat ingredients together thoroughly in a bowl.

3 Cut one-third off the pastry and reserve it for the lattice. Roll out the remainder and use it to line a 9 in, loose-based cake pan. Take care to push the pastry well into the edges and make a ¼ in rim around the top edge.

4 With a rolling pin, roll off the excess pastry to neaten the edge. Fill the pastry crust with the mincemeat.

5 Roll out the remaining pastry and cut it into ½ in strips. Arrange the strips in a lattice over the top of the pastry, wet the joins and press them together well. Chill for 30 minutes.

6 Preheat the oven to 375°F. Place a baking sheet in the oven to preheat. Brush the pastry with water and dust it with superfine sugar. Bake it on the baking sheet for 30–40 minutes. Transfer to a wire rack and let cool for 15 minutes. Then carefully remove the cake pan. Serve warm or cold, with sweetened, whipped cream.

Iced Praline Torte

Make this elaborate torte several days ahead, decorate it and return it to the freezer until you are nearly ready to serve it. Allow the torte to stand at room temperature for an hour before serving, or leave it in the refrigerator overnight to soften.

Serves 8

INGREDIENTS
1 cup almonds or hazelnuts
8 tbsp superfine sugar
⅔ cup raisins
6 tbsp rum or brandy
4 oz dark chocolate, broken into squares
2 tbsp milk
1⅞ cups heavy cream
2 tbsp strong black coffee
16 ladyfinger cookies

TO FINISH
⅔ cup heavy cream
½ cup slivered almonds, toasted
½ oz dark chocolate, melted

cookies

heavy cream

dark chocolate

black coffee

almonds

raisins

brandy

1 To make the praline, have ready an oiled cake pan or baking sheet. Put the nuts into a heavy-based pan with the sugar and heat gently until the sugar melts. Swirl the pan to coat the nuts in the hot sugar. Cook slowly until the nuts brown and the sugar caramelizes. Watch all the time, as this will only take a few minutes. Turn the nuts quickly into the pan or on to the tray and let them cool completely. Break them up and grind them to a fine powder in a food processor.

2 Soak the raisins in 3 tbsp of the rum or brandy for an hour (or better still overnight), so they soften and absorb the rum. Melt the chocolate with the milk in a bowl over a pan of hot, but not boiling water. Remove and let cool. Lightly grease a 5 cup loaf pan and line it with wax paper.

3 Whisk the cream in a bowl until it holds soft peaks. Whisk in the cold chocolate. Then fold in the praline and the soaked raisins, with any liquid.

4 Mix the coffee and remaining rum or brandy in a shallow dish. Dip in the ladyfingers and arrange half in a layer over the base of the prepared loaf pan.

5 Cover with the chocolate mixture and add another layer of soaked ladyfingers. Freeze overnight.

6 Dip the pan briefly into warm water to loosen the torte and turn it out on to a serving plate. Cover with whipped cream. Sprinkle the top with toasted slivered almonds and drizzle the melted chocolate over the top. Return the torte to the freezer until it's needed.

Spiced Pears in Red Wine

Serve these pears hot or cold, with lightly whipped cream. The flavors improve with keeping, so you can make this several days before you want it.

Serves 8

INGREDIENTS
2½ cups red wine
1⅛ cups superfine sugar
2½ in cinnamon stick
6 cloves
finely grated rind of 1 orange
2 tsp grated ginger root
8 even-sized firm pears, with stems
1 tbsp brandy
2 tbsp almonds or hazelnuts, toasted,
    to decorate

red wine

superfine sugar

pears

orange

brandy

almonds

cinnamon sticks

1 Choose a pan large enough to hold all the pears upright in one layer. Put all the ingredients except the pears, brandy and almonds into the pan and heat slowly until the sugar has dissolved. Simmer for 5 minutes.

2 Peel the pears, leaving the stems on, and cut away the flower end. Arrange them upright in the pan. Cover with a lid and simmer *very* gently until they are tender. The cooking time will vary depending on their size and how ripe they are, but will be about 45–50 minutes.

3 Remove the pears from the syrup with a slotted spoon, being careful not to pull out the stems. Put them in a serving bowl or individual bowls.

4 Bring the syrup to a boil and boil it rapidly until it thickens and reduces. Let cool slightly, add the brandy and strain over the pears. Sprinkle on the toasted nuts to decorate.

Frozen Grand Marnier Soufflés

These sophisticated little desserts are always appreciated and make a wonderful end to a special meal.

Serves 8

INGREDIENTS
1 cup superfine sugar
6 large eggs, separated
1 cup milk
½ oz powdered gelatin, soaked in
   3 tbsp cold water
1⅞ cups heavy cream
4 tbsp Grand Marnier

cream

Grand Marnier

eggs

superfine sugar

gelatin

1 Tie a double-collar of wax paper around eight ramekins. Put 6 tbsp of the sugar in a bowl with the egg yolks and whisk until pale.

2 Heat the milk until almost boiling and pour it on to the yolks, whisking all the time. Return to the pan and stir it over a gentle heat until it is thick enough to coat the spoon. Remove the pan from the heat. Stir the soaked gelatin into the custard. Pour into a bowl and leave to cool. Whisk occasionally, until the custard is on the point of setting.

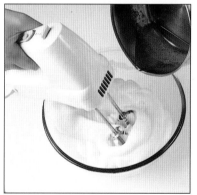

3 Put the remaining sugar in a pan with the water and dissolve it over a low heat. Bring to a boil and boil rapidly until it reaches the soft ball stage or 240°F on a sugar thermometer. Remove from the heat. In a clean bowl, whisk the egg whites until they are stiff. Pour the hot syrup on to the whites, whisking all the time. Let cool.

4 Whisk the cream until it holds soft peaks. Add the Grand Marnier to the cold custard and fold the custard into the cold meringue, with the cream. Quickly pour into the prepared ramekins. Freeze overnight. Remove the paper collars. Leave the soufflés at room temperature for 30 minutes before serving.

White Amaretto Mousses with Chocolate Sauce

These little desserts are extremely rich, and derive their flavor from Amaretto, an almond-flavored liqueur, and amaretti, little almond-flavored cookies.

Serves 8

INGREDIENTS
4 oz amaretti or macaroon
   cookies
4 tbsp Amaretto liqueur
12 oz white chocolate, broken into
   squares
½ oz powdered gelatin, soaked in
   3 tbsp cold water
1⅞ cups heavy cream

FOR THE CHOCOLATE SAUCE
8 oz dark chocolate, broken into
   squares
1¼ cups light cream
4 tbsp superfine sugar

cream

amaretti cookies

Amaretto

white chocolate

dark chocolate

superfine sugar

1 Lightly oil eight individual 4 fl oz molds and line the base of each mold with a small disc of oiled wax paper. Put the cookies into a large bowl and crush them finely with a rolling pin.

2 Melt the Amaretto and white chocolate together gently in a bowl over a pan of hot but not boiling water (be very careful not to overheat the chocolate). Stir well until smooth; remove from the pan and let cool.

3 Melt the gelatin over hot water and blend it into the chocolate mixture. Whisk the cream until it holds soft peaks. Fold in the chocolate mixture, with 4 tbsp of the crushed cookies.

4 Put a teaspoonful of the crushed cookies into the bottom of each mold and spoon in the chocolate mixture. Tap each mold to disperse any air bubbles. Level the tops and sprinkle the remaining crushed cookies on top. Press down gently and chill for 4 hours.

5 To make the chocolate sauce, put all the ingredients in a small pan and heat gently to melt the chocolate and dissolve the sugar. Simmer for 2–3 minutes. Let cool completely.

6 Slip a knife around the sides of each mold, and turn out on to individual plates. Remove the wax paper and pour round a little dark chocolate sauce.

Crunchy Apple and Almond Flan

Do not be tempted to put any sugar with the apples, as this makes them produce too much liquid. All the sweetness is in the pastry and topping.

Serves 8

INGREDIENTS
6 tbsp butter
1½ cups all-purpose flour
scant ⅓ cup ground almonds
2 tbsp superfine sugar
1 egg yolk
1 tbsp cold water
¼ tsp almond extract
sifted confectioner's sugar, to
    decorate

FOR THE CRUNCHY TOPPING
1 cup all-purpose flour
¼ tsp ground allspice
4 tbsp butter, cut in small cubes
4 tbsp demerara sugar
½ cup slivered almonds

FOR THE FILLING
1½ lb apples
2 tbsp raisins or sultanas

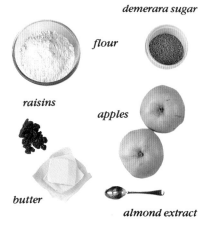

demerara sugar

flour

raisins

apples

butter

almond extract

1 To make the pastry, rub the butter, by hand or in a processor, into the flour until it resembles fine bread crumbs. Stir in the ground almonds and sugar. Whisk the egg yolk, water and almond extract together and mix them into the dry ingredients to form a soft, pliable dough. Knead the dough lightly until smooth, wrap in plastic wrap and leave in a cool place to rest for 20 minutes.

4 Roll off the excess pastry to neaten the edge. Chill for 15 minutes.

2 Meanwhile, make the crunchy topping Sift the flour and allspice into a bowl and rub in the butter. Stir in the sugar and almonds.

5 Preheat the oven to 375°F. Place a baking sheet in the oven to preheat. Peel, core and slice the apples thinly. Arrange the slices in the crust in overlapping, concentric circles, doming the center. Scatter the raisins or sultanas over. The flan will seem too full at this stage, but as the apples cook the filling will drop slightly.

3 Roll out the pastry on a lightly floured surface and use it to line a 9 in loose-based cake pan, taking care to press it neatly into the edges and to make a lip around the top edge.

6 Cover the apples with the crunchy topping mixture, pressing it on lightly. Bake on the hot baking sheet for 25–30 minutes, or until the top is golden brown and the apples are tender (test them with a fine skewer). Let the flan cool in the pan for 10 minutes. Serve warm or cold, dusted with sifted confectioner's sugar.

Moist and Rich Christmas Cake

The cake can be made 4–6 weeks before Christmas. During this time, pierce the cake with a fine needle and spoon over 2–3 tbsp brandy.

Makes 1 × 8 in cake

INGREDIENTS
1⅓ cups sultanas
1 cup currants
1⅓ cups raisins
4 oz prunes, pitted and chopped
¼ cup candied cherries, halved
⅓ cup mixed candied citrus peel, chopped
3 tbsp brandy or sherry
2 cups all-purpose flour
pinch of salt
½ tsp ground cinnamon
½ tsp grated nutmeg
1 tbsp cocoa powder
1 cup butter
1 generous cup dark brown sugar
4 large eggs
finely grated rind of 1 orange or lemon
⅔ cup ground almonds
½ cup chopped almonds

TO DECORATE
4 tbsp apricot jam
10 in round cake board
1 lb almond paste
1 lb white fondant icing
8 oz royal icing
1½ yd ribbon

sultanas

flour

butter

almonds

currants

candied cherries

prunes

nutmeg

cinnamon

cocoa powder

citrus peel

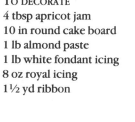
The day before you want to bake the cake, put all the dried fruit to soak in the brandy or sherry, cover it with plastic wrap and leave overnight. Grease a 8 in round cake pan and line it with a double thickness of wax paper.

2 The next day, preheat the oven to 325°F. Sift together the flour, salt, spices and cocoa powder. Whisk the butter and sugar together until light and fluffy and beat in the eggs gradually. Finally mix in the orange or lemon rind, the ground and chopped almonds and the dried fruits (with any liquid). Fold the flour mixture into the dried fruit mixture.

4 Warm then sieve the apricot jam to make a glaze. Remove the paper from the cake and place it in the center of the cake board and brush it with hot apricot glaze. Cover the cake with a layer of almond paste and then a layer of fondant icing. Pipe a border around the base of the cake with royal icing. Tie a ribbon around the sides.

3 Spoon into the prepared cake pan, level the top and give the cake pan a gentle tap on the work surface to settle the mixture and disperse any air bubbles. Bake for 3 hours, or until a fine skewer inserted into the middle comes out clean. Transfer the cake pan to a wire rack and let the cake cool in the pan for an hour. Then carefully turn the cake out on to the wire rack, but leave the paper on, as it will help to keep the cake moist during storage. When the cake is cold, wrap it tightly in foil and store it in a cool place.

5 Roll out any trimmings from the fondant icing and stamp out 12 small holly leaves with a cutter. Make one bell motif with a cookie mold, dusted first with sifted confectioner's sugar. Roll 36 small balls for the holly berries. Leave on wax paper to dry for 24 hours. Decorate the cake with the leaves, berries and bell, attaching them with a little royal icing.

Nut and Candied Fruit Ring

The cake can be made two or three weeks before Christmas. Store it in a tin in a cool place until needed.

Makes 1 × 9 in ring

INGREDIENTS
½ cup candied cherries, quartered
⅓ cup raisins or sultanas
4 oz dried apricots, quartered
4 oz dried prunes, pitted and
    quartered
½ cup pitted and chopped dates
4 tbsp rum, brandy or sherry
½ cup butter
½ cup dark brown sugar
½ tsp ground cinnamon
½ tsp ground allspice
2 eggs, beaten
⅔ cup ground almonds
1 cup coarsely chopped walnuts
2 cups self-rising flour

TO FINISH
2 tbsp rum, brandy or sherry
4 tbsp apricot jam
whole blanched almonds, split
3 candied cherries, halved
few strips angelica

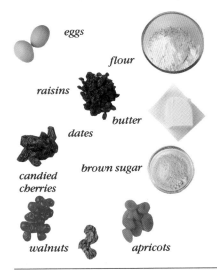

eggs

flour

raisins

butter

dates

brown sugar

candied
cherries

walnuts   apricots

1 The day before you want to bake the cake, soak all the dried fruit in the rum, brandy or sherry. Cover with plastic wrap and leave overnight. Grease a 9 in ring mold, with a 6¼ cup capacity.

2 The next day, preheat the oven to 325°F. In a large bowl, whisk the butter, sugar and spices together until they are light and fluffy. Whisk in the eggs, and then fold in the drained, soaked fruits, with any liquid. Mix in the ground almonds, walnuts and flour.

3 Spoon the mixture into the prepared cake pan, level the top and bake for 1½–2 hours. Let cool in the tin for 30 minutes then turn out on to a wire rack to cool completely. Brush with the rum, brandy or sherry.

4 Put the apricot jam in a small pan and heat it gently to melt it. Strain the jam. Brush the hot glaze over the top of the cake. Arrange the nuts and fruit in a flower design on top of the cake and brush them liberally with more apricot glaze, which must be used very hot, or the decoration will lift while you are brushing the jam over it.

Light Jeweled Fruit Cake

If you want to cover the cake with marzipan and icing omit the whole-almond decoration. The cake can be made up to two weeks before eating it. For serving, brush the top with hot apricot jam and tie a pretty ribbon around the sides.

Makes 1 × 8 in cake

INGREDIENTS
½ cup currants
⅔ cup sultanas
1 cup candied cherries (mixed red, green and yellow), quartered
⅓ cup mixed candied citrus peel, finely chopped
2 tbsp rum, brandy or sherry
1 cup butter
1⅛ cups superfine sugar
finely grated rind of 1 orange
finely grated rind of 1 lemon
4 eggs
½ cup chopped almonds
⅔ cup ground almonds
2 cups all-purpose flour

TO FINISH
2 oz whole blanched almonds (optional)
1 tbsp apricot jam

peel

candied cherries

ground almonds

sultanas
butter

orange

lemon

eggs

flour

1 The day before you want to bake the cake, soak the currants, sultanas, candied cherries and the mixed peel in the rum, brandy or sherry. Cover with plastic wrap and leave overnight. The next day, grease and line an 8 in round cake pan or a 7 in square cake pan with a double thickness of wax paper.

2 Preheat the oven to 325°F. In a large bowl, whisk the butter, sugar and orange and lemon rinds together until they are light and fluffy. Beat in the eggs, one at a time.

3 Mix in the chopped almonds, ground almonds, soaked fruits (with their liquid) and the flour, to make a soft dropping consistency. Spoon into the cake pan and level the top. Bake for 30 minutes.

4 Arrange the whole almonds in a pattern on top of the cake. Do not press them into the cake or they will sink during cooking. Return the cake to the oven and cook for a further 1½–2 hours, or until the center is firm to the touch. Let the cake cool in the pan for 30 minutes. Then remove it and let it cool completely on a wire rack, but leave the paper on, as it helps to keep the cake moist while it is stored. When cold, wrap the cake in foil and store it in a cool place. Remove the paper before serving, and heat then strain the apricot jam. Brush the glaze over the cake. Let cool.

Passion Cake

A complete change from the traditional rich Christmas cake. The icing thickens quickly as it cools and will become difficult to spread, so have the cake on a serving plate and a spatula ready to spread the icing once it is ready. The cake will stay moist for days.

Serves 8

INGREDIENTS
10 tbsp butter
scant 1 cup light brown sugar
2 eggs, beaten
6 oz carrots, finely grated
finely grated rind of 1 orange
large pinch of salt
1 tsp ground cinnamon
½ tsp grated nutmeg
1¾ cups self-rising flour
1 tsp baking powder
⅔ cup raisins
½ cup chopped walnuts
2 tbsp milk

FOR THE ICING
2¼ cups granulated sugar
⅔ cup water
pinch of cream of tartar
2 egg whites

flour

carrots

orange

butter

walnuts

brown sugar

eggs

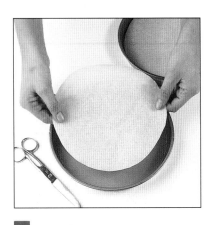

1 Preheat the oven to 375°F. Grease and line the bases of two 8 in square cake pans.

2 In a bowl, whisk together the butter and sugar until pale and fluffy. Beat in the eggs gradually, and then stir in the remaining ingredients to make a soft dropping consistency.

3 Spoon the mixture into the prepared cake pans and bake for 25–30 minutes, or until the cakes are firm to the touch. Let the cakes cool in the pans for 5 minutes. Then turn out on to a wire rack and let cool completely.

4 For the icing, put the sugar and water in a pan and heat them very gently to dissolve the sugar. (Swirl the pan to mix the sugar, do not stir it with a spoon.) Add the cream of tartar and bring to a boil. Boil to 240°F or to the soft ball stage. Quickly dip the base of the pan in cold water. Whisk the egg whites until they are stiff and pour the syrup over them, whisking all the time. Continue whisking until the icing loses its satiny appearance and will hold its shape. Quickly sandwich the cakes with the icing and spread the rest over the cake.

Almond Mincemeat Tartlets

These little tartlets are a welcome change from traditional mince pies. Serve them warm with brandy- or rum-flavored custard. They freeze well and can be reheated for serving.

Makes 36

INGREDIENTS
2½ cups all-purpose flour
generous ¾ cup confectioner's sugar
1 tsp ground cinnamon
¾ cup butter
⅔ cup ground almonds
1 egg yolk
3 tbsp milk
1 lb jar mincemeat
1 tbsp brandy or rum

FOR THE LEMON SPONGE FILLING
½ cup butter or margarine
8 tbsp superfine sugar
1½ cups self-rising flour
2 large eggs
finely grated rind of 1 large lemon

FOR THE LEMON ICING
1 generous cup confectioner's sugar
1 tbsp lemon juice

butter

flour

brandy

eggs

confectioner's sugar

mincemeat

ground almonds

1 For the pastry, sift the flour, icing sugar and cinnamon into a bowl or a food processor and rub in the butter until it resembles fine bread crumbs. Add the ground almonds and bind with the egg yolk and milk to a soft, pliable dough. Knead the dough until smooth, wrap it in plastic wrap and chill it for 30 minutes.

2 Preheat the oven to 375°F. On a lightly floured surface, roll out the pastry and cut out 36 fluted rounds, to line the patty pans, with a pastry cutter. Mix the mincemeat with the brandy or rum and put a small teaspoonful in the bottom of each crust. Chill for 10 minutes.

3 For the lemon sponge filling, whisk the butter or margarine, sugar, flour, eggs and lemon rind together until smooth. Spoon on top of the mincemeat, dividing it evenly, and level the tops. Bake for 20–30 minutes, or until golden brown and springy to the touch. Remove and let cool on a wire rack.

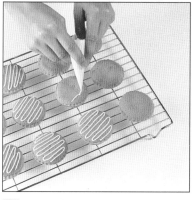

4 For the lemon icing, sift the confectioner's sugar and mix with the lemon juice to a smooth, thick, coating consistency. Spoon into a piping bag and drizzle a zigzag pattern over each tart. If you're short of time, simply dust the tartlets with sifted confectioner's sugar.

Christmas Cookies

These are great fun for children to make as presents. Any shape of cookie cutter can be used. Store them in an airtight tin. For a change, omit the lemon rind and add ⅓ cup of ground almonds and a few drops of almond extract.

Makes about 12

INGREDIENTS
6 tbsp butter
generous ½ cup confectioner's sugar
finely grated rind of 1 small lemon
1 egg yolk
1½ cups all-purpose flour
pinch of salt

TO DECORATE
2 egg yolks
red and green edible food coloring

1 In a large bowl, beat the butter, sugar and lemon rind together until pale and fluffy. Beat in the egg yolk, and then sift in the flour and the salt. Knead together to form a smooth dough. Wrap in plastic wrap and chill for 30 minutes.

flour

confectioner's sugar

butter

eggs

food coloring

lemon

2 Preheat the oven to 375°F. On a lightly floured surface, roll out the dough to ⅛ in thick. Using a 2½ in fluted cutter, stamp out as many cookies as you can, with the cutter dipped in flour to prevent it from sticking to the dough.

3 Transfer the cookies on to lightly greased baking trays. Mark the tops lightly with a 1 in holly leaf cutter and use a ¼ in plain piping nozzle for the berries. Chill for 10 minutes, until firm.

4 Meanwhile, put each egg yolk into a small cup. Mix red food coloring into one and green food coloring into the other. Using a small, clean paintbrush, carefully paint the colors on to the cookies. Bake the cookies for 10–12 minutes, or until they begin to color around the edges. Let them cool slightly on the baking trays, and then transfer them to a wire rack to cool completely.

Shortbread

You can also roll the dough out and cut it into fluted rounds, or press it into an 7 in tin and cut it into bars.

Makes 1 × 8 in round

INGREDIENTS
½ cup butter
4 tbsp superfine sugar, plus extra to decorate
1½ cups all-purpose flour
pinch of salt
24 whole blanched almonds, to decorate (optional)

butter

flour

superfine sugar

almonds

1 Preheat the oven to 325°F. In a large bowl, beat together the butter and sugar until smooth and fluffy. Mix in the flour and a pinch of salt until the mixture resembles fine bread crumbs.

2 With your hands, gather the mixture together to form a smooth dough (handle it as little as possible or the butter begins to become oily).

3 Press the dough evenly into a 8 in loose-based cake pan (use your knuckles to press it firmly into the edges). Level the top with the back of a spoon.

4 Decorate the edge with the prongs of a fork and prick it all over. Cut the dough into wedges. Press in the almonds in a pattern, if you like. Bake for 40–50 minutes, or until the shortbread is a pale golden brown. Dust it with superfine sugar while still warm. Let it cool in the pan for a few minutes, and then transfer it to a wire rack to cool completely.

Ginger Florentines

These colorful, chewy cookies are delicious served with ice cream and are certain to disappear as soon as they are served. Store them in an airtight container.

Makes 30

INGREDIENTS
4 tbsp butter
8 tbsp superfine sugar
3 rounded tbsp mixed candied cherries, chopped
2 rounded tbsp candied orange peel, chopped
½ cup slivered almonds
½ cup chopped walnuts
1 tbsp crystallized ginger, chopped
2 tbsp all-purpose flour
½ tsp ground ginger

TO FINISH
2 oz dark chocolate, or chocolate chips, melted
2 oz white chocolate, or chocolate chips, melted

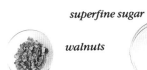 superfine sugar

walnuts

chocolate

 orange peel

candied cherries

 crystallized ginger

almonds

1 Preheat the oven to 350°F. Whisk the butter and sugar together until they are light and fluffy. Thoroughly mix in all the remaining ingredients, except the melted chocolate.

2 Cut a piece of non-stick baking parchment to fit your baking trays. Put 4 small spoonfuls of the mixture on to each tray, spacing them well apart to allow for spreading. Flatten the cookies and bake them for 5 minutes.

3 Remove the cookies from the oven and flatten them with a wet fork, shaping them into neat rounds. Return to the oven for 3–4 minutes, until they are golden brown.

4 Let them cool on the baking trays for 2 minutes, to firm up, and then carefully transfer them to a wire rack. When they are cold and firm, spread the melted dark chocolate on the undersides of half the biscuits and spread the melted white chocolate on the undersides of the rest.

Chocolate Kisses

These rich little cookies look pretty mixed together on a plate and dusted with confectioner's sugar. Serve them with ice cream or simply with coffee.

Makes 24

INGREDIENTS
3 oz dark chocolate, broken into
   squares
3 oz white chocolate, broken into
   squares
½ cup butter
8 tbsp superfine sugar
2 eggs
2 cups all-purpose flour
confectioner's sugar, to decorate

confectioner's sugar

flour

butter

eggs

chocolate

1 Put each chocolate into a small bowl and melt it over a pan of hot, but not boiling, water. Set aside to cool.

2 Whisk together the butter and confectioner's sugar until they are pale and fluffy. Beat in the eggs, one at a time. Then sift in the flour and mix well.

3 Halve the mixture and divide it between the two bowls of chocolate. Mix each chocolate in thoroughly. Knead the doughs until smooth, wrap them in plastic wrap and chill them for 1 hour. Preheat the oven to 375°F.

4 Shape slightly rounded teaspoonfuls of both doughs roughly into balls. Roll the balls in the palms of your hands to make neater ball shapes. Arrange the balls on greased baking sheets and bake them for 10–12 minutes. Dust with sifted confectioner's sugar and then transfer them to a wire rack to cool.

Filo Crackers

These can be prepared a day in advance, brushed with melted butter and kept covered with plastic wrap in the fridge or freezer before baking.

Makes about 24

INGREDIENTS
2 × 10 oz packet frozen filo pastry, thawed
½ cup butter, melted
thin silver ribbon, to decorate
sifted confectioner's sugar, to decorate

FOR THE FILLING
1 lb apples, peeled, cored and finely chopped
1 tsp ground cinnamon
2 tbsp light brown sugar
½ cup pecans, chopped
1 cup fresh white bread crumbs
3 tbsp sultanas
3 heaping tbsp currants

FOR THE LEMON SAUCE
4 oz superfine sugar
finely grated rind of 1 lemon
juice of 2 lemons

filo pastry

brown sugar

superfine sugar

lemons

1 Unwrap the filo pastry and cover it with plastic wrap and a damp cloth, to prevent it from drying out. Put the chopped apples in a bowl and mix in the remaining filling ingredients.

2 Take one sheet of pastry at a time and cut it into 6 × 12 in strips. Brush with butter. Place a spoonful of the filling at one end and fold in the sides so the pastry measures 5 in across. Brush the edges with butter and roll up. Pinch the 'frill' at either end and tie with ribbon. Brush with butter.

3 Place the crackers on baking sheets, cover and chill for 10 minutes. Preheat the oven to 375°F. Brush each cracker with melted butter. Bake the crackers for 30–35 minutes, or until they are golden brown. Let them cool slightly on the baking trays and then transfer them to a wire rack to cool completely.

4 To make the lemon sauce, put all the ingredients in a small pan and heat gently to dissolve the sugar. Serve the sauce warm, in a pitcher. Finally, dust the crackers with sifted confectioner's sugar and arrange them on a serving plate.